COMMON ENTRANCE • K

CE 13+

English

Exam Practice
Questions
and Answers

About the authors

Amanda Alexander and Rachel Gee have extensive experience in teaching and managing in both state and private schools. They are friends and colleagues and approached Galore Park with publishing ideas as they were frustrated with English textbook resources on the market at that time.

They have a wealth of knowledge and considerable expertise in teaching English and preparing children for English at 13+, which they bring to this book. They are the authors of all the editions of the successful *English Practice Exercises 13+*. In their spare time, they still meet to enjoy a walk and discuss the joys (and maybe some frustrations) of teaching, and life in general.

Text credits

P9 Esther Hautzig (1993), *The Endless Steppe,* Puffin (Penguin); **P13** Tracy Chevalier (2009), *The Girl with a Pearl Earring*, HarperCollins; **P22** Tara Westover (2018), *Educated*, Windmill Books (Penguin); **P27** Cornelia Funke (2010), *Reckless*, Pushkin Children's Books (Pushkin Press); **P32** Carlos Ruiz Zafón (2004), *The Shadow of the Wind*, W&N (Orion); **P36** Liz Lochhead (1972), 'The Choosing' from *A Choosing*, Birlinn (Polygon); **P41** Simon Armitage (2007), *Sir Gawain and the Green Knight*, Faber & Faber; **P50** Benjamin Zephaniah/Lemn Sissay (2013), *Refugee Boy*, Methuen Drama (Bloomsbury); **P55** JB Priestley (1945), *An Inspector Calls*, Heinemann (Penguin); **P60** Alan Bennett (1968), *Forty Years* On, Faber & Faber

Although every effort has been made to ensure that website addresses are correct at time of going to press, Galore Park cannot be held responsible for the content of any website mentioned in this book. It is sometimes possible to find a relocated web page by typing in the address of the home page for a website in the URL window of your browser.

Hachette UK's policy is to use papers that are natural, renewable and recyclable products and made from wood grown in well-managed forests and other controlled sources. The logging and manufacturing processes are expected to conform to the environmental regulations of the country of origin.

Orders: please contact Hachette UK Distribution, Hely Hutchinson Centre, Milton Road, Didcot, Oxfordshire, OX11 7HH. Telephone: (44) 01235 400555. Lines are open from 9 a.m. to 5 p.m., Monday to Friday. Email: primary@hachette.co.uk

Parents, Tutors please call: (44) 02031 226405 (Monday to Friday, 9:30 a.m. to 4:30 p.m.).

Email: parentenquiries@galorepark.co.uk

Visit our website at www.galorepark.co.uk for details of revision guides for Common Entrance, examination papers and Galore Park publications.

ISBN: 978 1 3983 26484

© Hodder & Stoughton 2022
First published in 2022 by Hodder & Stoughton Limited
An Hachette UK Company
Carmelite House
50 Victoria Embankment
London EC4Y 0DZ
www.galorepark.co.uk

Impression number 10 9 8 7 6 5 4 3 2

Year 2026 2025 2024 2023

All rights reserved. Apart from any use permitted under UK copyright law, no part of this publication may be reproduced or transmitted in any form or by any means, electronic or mechanical, including photocopying and recording, or held within any information storage and retrieval system, without permission in writing from the publisher or under licence from the Copyright Licensing Agency Limited. Further details of such licences (for reprographic reproduction) may be obtained from the Copyright Licensing Agency Limited, www.cla.co.uk

Illustrations by Aptara, Inc.

Typeset in India

Printed by CPI Group (UK) Ltd, Croydon CR0 4YY

A catalogue record for this title is available from the British Library

Contents

Introduction	4
Exam practice questions	5
Foundation and Paper 1 (Reading): Practice Papers	6
Introduction	6
Foundation: Practice Paper 1: *The Endless Steppe* (Esther Hautzig)	9
Foundation: Practice Paper 2: *The Girl with a Pearl Earring* (Tracy Chevalier)	13
Foundation: Practice Paper 3: *The Adventures of Tom Sawyer* (Mark Twain)	18
Paper 1 (Reading): Prose Practice Paper 1: *Educated* (Tara Westover)	22
Paper 1 (Reading): Prose Practice Paper 2: *Reckless* (Cornelia Funke)	27
Paper 1 (Reading): Prose Practice Paper 3: *The Shadow of the Wind* (Carlos Ruiz Zafón)	32
Paper 1 (Reading): Poetry Practice Paper 1: 'The Choosing' (Liz Lochhead)	36
Paper 1 (Reading): Poetry Practice Paper 2: 'Sir Gawain and the Green Knight' (Simon Armitage)	41
Paper 1 (Reading): Poetry Practice Paper 3: From 'Snake' (DH Lawrence)	45
Paper 1 (Reading): Drama Practice Paper 1: *Refugee Boy* (Benjamin Zephaniah/Lemn Sissay)	50
Paper 1 (Reading): Drama Practice Paper 2: *An Inspector Calls* (JB Priestley)	55
Paper 1 (Reading): Drama Practice Paper 3: *Forty Years On* (Alan Bennett)	60
Paper 2 Writing: Practice Papers	65
Introduction	65
A guide to styles and forms	65
Writing strategies and tips	65
Planning your responses	66
Checking your work carefully	67
Writing Practice Papers	68
Exam practice answers	74
Foundation and Paper 1 (Reading): Practice Paper Answers	75
Guidance for students, teachers and parents	75
Foundation: Practice Paper 1: *The Endless Steppe*	76
Foundation: Practice Paper 2: *The Girl with a Pearl Earring*	80
Foundation: Practice Paper 3: *The Adventures of Tom Sawyer*	83
Paper 1 (Reading): Prose Practice Paper 1: *Educated*	87
Paper 1 (Reading): Prose Practice Paper 2: *Reckless*	92
Paper 1 (Reading): Prose Practice Paper 3: *The Shadow of the Wind*	96
Paper 1 (Reading): Poetry Practice Paper 1: 'The Choosing'	102
Paper 1 (Reading): Poetry Practice Paper 2: 'Sir Gawain and the Green Knight'	107
Paper 1 (Reading): Poetry Practice Paper 3: From 'Snake'	112
Paper 1 (Reading): Drama Practice Paper 1: *Refugee Boy*	117
Paper 1 (Reading): Drama Practice Paper 2: *An Inspector Calls*	123
Paper 1 (Reading): Drama Practice Paper 3: *Forty Years On*	129
Paper 2 Writing: Practice Paper Answers	135
Guidance for students, teachers and parents	135
Sample responses to a range of writing styles and forms	141
Appendix: Subject content from ISEB English 13+ specification	153

Introduction

We welcome you to our book and hope it helps you to approach the 13+ English exams with confidence. Whether you usually enjoy reading or not, the reading comprehension extracts we have chosen may whet your appetite, and be both thought-provoking and of interest. There are many reading and writing skills to practise and develop, and by using the answer section, in conjunction with the question papers, you will get a better insight into the examiner's expectations. If you make mistakes along the way, use these to your advantage and learn from them. As you progress, give yourself a pat on the back and have the confidence to realise that there may be more than one answer.

The ISEB is looking for:

- the 'development of a confident and engaging personal voice'
  As you develop your responses to comprehension and writing tasks, try to find your own confident voice so that you stand out as an individual to the examiner.
- an 'appreciation of writers' craft; development of expression in pupils' own writing'
  These extracts are all well-written. Although you may prefer some to others, try always to admire the authors' 'craft' and practise using the same skills to discover which work for you.
- 'confidence and accuracy in spelling, punctuation and grammar, so that writing is clear, accurate and coherent'
  The point of this necessary accuracy is to ensure that your writing is clear for your examiner.
- an 'adaptation of language, form and tone, according to purpose and audience'
  Read the question carefully and deliver what is asked for. Choose your language to suit your task and reader (your examiner or the task's audience).
- the 'written articulation of a well-structured, independent and critical response to literature'.
  Hopefully, your outcome, whether comprehension or writing, will be clearly structured showing independent thought.

Enjoy the journey.

What you have to do – the specification

As described in the ISEB specification (see the Appendix) candidates are required to respond to reading and writing tasks over two papers.

This book contains Foundation Reading and Paper 1 (Reading) practice exercises. It also contains Paper 2 Writing exercises which are common to both levels (Foundation and Paper 1).

Foundation Reading papers may be used for assessment at 13+ or to provide familiarisation and an introduction to Paper 1 (Reading).

The answer section at the back of the book provides additional advice for the teacher and parent but also enables students to understand the final expectation and so monitor their own progress.

You can also find much more detail of what the ISEB requires in the Appendix of subject content from the ISEB 13+ English specification: **www.iseb.co.uk/Schools/Examination-syllabuses-specimen-papers/New-CE-at-13**.

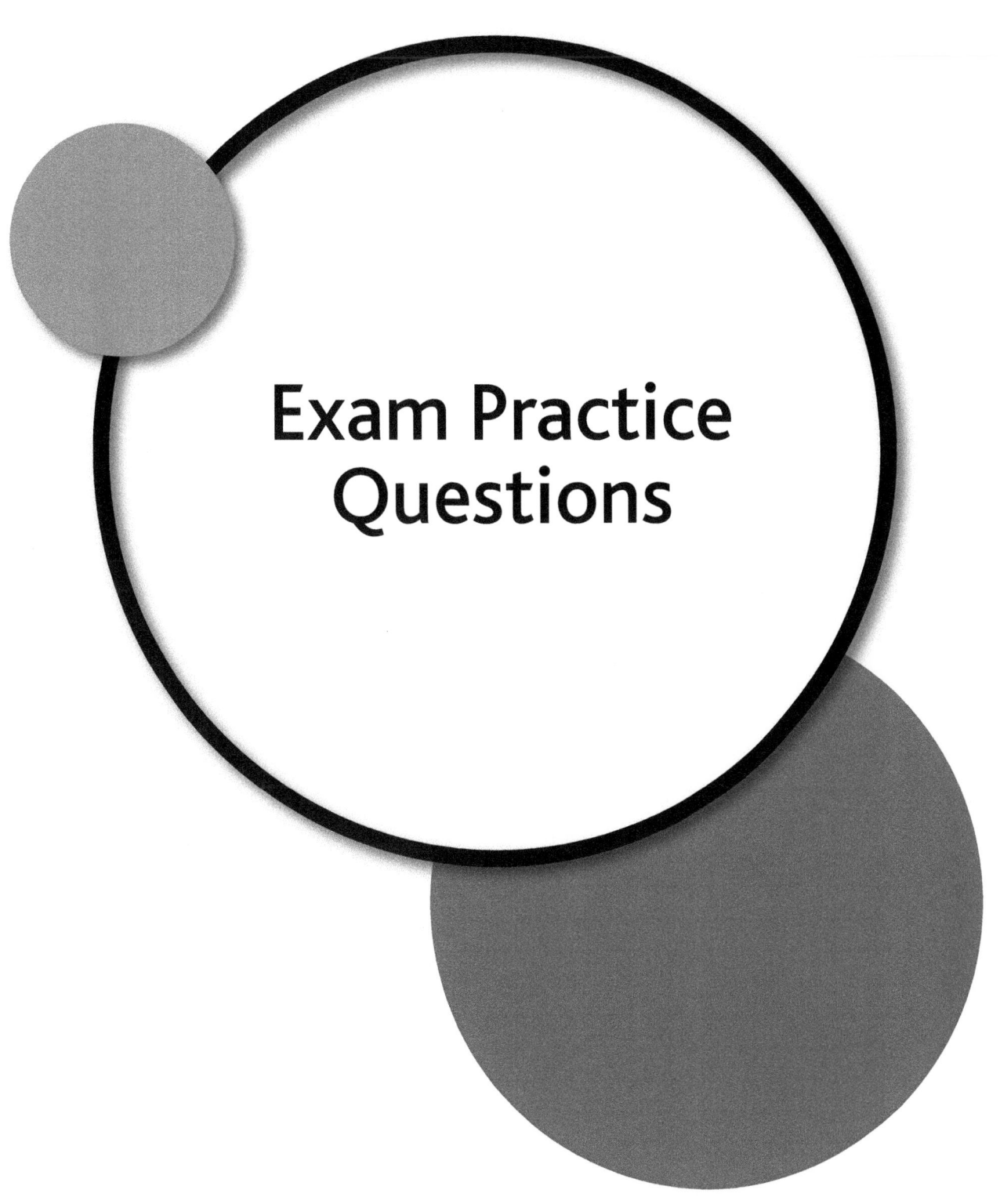

Foundation and Paper 1 (Reading): Practice Papers

Introduction
The texts and questions are all designed to respond to the requirements of the specification to be first examined in November 2022.

Foundation
This section of the book may be used for developing the skills and vocabulary for Paper 1, as practice for assessment at 13+ or to support learning in Years 6 and 7. The text extract will always be a narrative prose passage.

Paper 1 (Reading)
This section of the book provides specific practice for assessment at 13+. The text extract will be either literary prose, poetry or drama. Within each genre these papers are graded in difficulty.

Timing
The ISEB 13+ Foundation and Paper 1 (Reading) question paper states: 'time allowed is 1 hour 10 minutes' for all three reading sections.

You will find that Section A enables you to familiarise yourself with the text; Section B builds on this in more detail; by the time you get to Section C you will be very familiar with the text. Initially, the paper may appear quite daunting, but each section provides a scaffold for the next.

How to read the exam extract
This is a reading test so give the text the time it needs and do not be in a rush to start your answers. Block out any distractions and do not feel pressure to start writing, even if others around you do so.

The texts will often be preceded by an introduction. This needs to be read carefully as it may help to prepare and unlock your understanding of the text. Do not be tempted to miss out or gloss over it.

Note that in the ISEB papers, difficult words have a number beside them and they are explained at the end of the extract. In this book these words are defined in callouts beside the extracts.

Foundation
The texts need a careful and thoughtful reading. Try to imagine yourself in the story. If you have a good understanding at this stage, it will save you time when answering the questions.

Paper 1
Literary prose – try to imagine yourself within the narrative.

Poetry – poems will need more than one reading in order to absorb the use of poetic techniques, rhythm, rhyme, structure and form. A careful reading will aid insightful understanding of the poem's 'feel' and all-important message.

Drama – as you read the extract, try to imagine the characters on the stage.

An understanding of the characters will be evident through what they say, do not say, how they react and how they are reacted to by others.

There may be stage directions, which will help you 'see' the action or setting and understand what the characters do and how they behave.

If you have a good understanding at this point, it will save you time when answering the questions.

How to tackle Section A
In this section there are eight multiple-choice questions, worth 15 marks.

Seven questions are worth 2 marks each; one question is worth 1 mark.

Introduction

The point of this section is to introduce you to the text, to guide you through it using careful reading and to clear up any misunderstandings.

Read the question carefully and take note of key words. The questions might test literal and general understanding, grammar, vocabulary and writing techniques.

Questions often follow the chronological order of the text. Take note of the line references, if there are any.

Read ALL the possible answers (a, b, c, d) to ensure that you find the closest match. If you are unsure, eliminate those that are definitely wrong.

Go back to the text to check your answer in context. It is best not to rely on memory. Do not snatch at an answer or jump to conclusions.

You may find that there is a question within this section where a written sentence response is required. Follow any instructions given.

How to tackle Section B

The questions in Section A provide a scaffold for these questions. There may be four or five questions in Section B worth a total of 25 marks.

These questions and answers require a deeper response using inferred understanding.

(See the answer section for further guidance on the mark allocation for the graded stages of response in some longer answers.)

You may prefer to read all these Section B questions first to ensure that you put the right information with the right question. A careful gathering of relevant detail is needed, with clear and developed explanations using the best evidence.

Again, key words and line references should be carefully underlined so that information is selected precisely.

The allocation of marks should be observed and used as a guide to understand the number of points needed and the level of detail required. (See the Reading Paper answer grids at the back of the book for further guidance.)

It may be necessary to think briefly through the structure of an answer and to find supporting quotations by highlighting the text (if allowed) before starting to write.

Unless directed otherwise, all Section B answers should be written in full sentences.

How to tackle Section C

Foundation

This section is just one question, worth 10 marks. Using your knowledge and understanding of the extract from Sections A and B, you will be asked to respond imaginatively and with feeling to the passage. This might be in the form of a story from another character's point of view or a continuation based on details within the extract.

Bring all your reading, understanding and writing skills to this section.

Use the bullets to help structure and plan your piece of writing. They are there to help you.

Paper 1

In this section there is just one question worth 10 marks. Using your knowledge and understanding of the extract from Sections A and B, you will be asked to consider the text as a whole.

Use the instructions to help you plan and direct your extended response. You will need to write three clearly demarcated paragraphs for this answer. Each paragraph should begin with a clear topic sentence stating the point of the argument. Then develop the response with linked explanations and discussion of evidence. Credit will be given to answers which show a deeper response to the analysis of language and form.

Keep an eye on the time (1 hour and 10 minutes) for the complete Reading Paper, allowing time to check at the end.

Foundation and Paper 1 (Reading): Practice Papers

Note that these exercises could also be used to practise key comprehension skills without the time pressure.

The answer section provides additional advice for the teacher and parent but also enables candidates to understand the final expectation and so monitor their progress.

Understanding the instruction on the front of the paper

On the ISEB 13+ Reading question papers, the following advice is given:

'Spelling, punctuation, grammar, vocabulary and presentation are all important and will be taken into account.'

Spelling

Take care to copy words accurately from the text. A careless approach may give the wrong impression. A good level of accuracy is expected, especially in the spelling of key literary terms.

Pay particular attention to the names of characters and places. The writer's name must be spelled correctly and referred to by the surname/the writer/the narrator/he/she/they.

Paper 1 candidates may also need to refer to the poet/the author/the playwright.

Punctuation

Capital letters and full stops should be clearly defined and correctly used.

It is important that quotations should be correctly punctuated. Punctuation within the quote should be copied exactly from the text and quotation marks either side of the quote should be evident and correctly placed.

Candidates should follow their schools' advice whether to use one or two quotation marks either side of the quotation.

A colon may be used to introduce a quotation.

An ellipsis, to indicate where words have been omitted, may be used to reduce the length of a quotation.

When quoting direct speech, the quotation marks and the speech marks should be evident:

'"That sounds ominous," casually remarked Father.'

'Father casually remarked, "That sounds ominous."'

'"That sounds ominous."'

Paper 1 candidates should remember to use a '/' to indicate a line break when quoting from the poem.

To get all this right in the exam will impress examiners.

Grammar

It is important to be a clear communicator. Sentences should be complete, accurate and formal with correct grammatical structures in place. For example, contractions (such as 'don't') should be avoided unless when quoting directly from the text extract or when writing dialogue in a Section C response.

Vocabulary

A clear, carefully chosen vocabulary aids a well-structured answer.

A variety of words may introduce or follow a quotation. For example, use 'shows', 'suggests', 'indicates' and 'proves'.

Technical words, specific to English, should be used with care and confidence.

Presentation

Handwriting should be consistently well-formed in a clear style with regular sizing and spacing. Crossing out should be limited and neat.

The Reading Papers which follow provide good opportunities to practise all these skills.

Foundation: Practice Paper 1

From *The Endless Steppe* by Esther Hautzig (1968)

> In the following extract, a young girl, Esther, goes to a new school in Russia when her family are exiled from Poland in 1941.

The morning I was to go to school for the first time, I woke up in a blackness as mysterious as the heart of a dark forest, the sounds nearby its strange beat. But the howl of a wolf way out in the country gave me my bearings.

I took up my little notebook and a small stub of pencil, my only academic possessions. How long would they last? How small could I write?

I quickly got dressed, as warmly as I could, although deep winter had not yet arrived. I pulled a sweater over my thin, little blouse, and struggled into my black leather shoes which were not only pinching but which were beginning to crack from the wet and the mud, and endless drying in front of our little stove. On went my one and only coat, I was ready to go.

Mother had to be at the bakery early that day and so, clutching my notebook and pencil, I went to school alone. It never occurred to me that for a child to walk alone down a deserted Siberian road, so obviously a stranger, required some courage. I was too busy trying to rehearse the Russian alphabet I would need to know in my new school.

In room number 5, a few children in caps and coats were seated at their desks watching the teacher write on the blackboard. She turned when I came in and looked at me so severely that my heart sank.

'You must be Esther Rudomin. From Poland. Your Russian will be poor.' It was as if she was reading from a dossier that would determine some sort of punishment. 'It will be my task to see that you improve it. My name is Raisa Nikitovna. Go to the last desk of the third row and sit down.'

Without another word, she picked up a book, and called out a page number. Everyone had a book but me. The feeling must have been something like a soldier without a gun. I leaned towards the girl next to me and asked if I might share her book. She grudgingly[1] agreed. She was a very pretty girl with short blond hair, and eyes the special blue of northern countries. I asked her name but she told me to be quiet; there was absolutely no talking in class.

My first lesson in school in Siberia was memorable for being a chilly one. It was not only the Russian author's meaning that evaded me, lost as it was in a sea of strange letters formed in the Russian alphabet, but so did the book itself – literally. My class mate somehow managed to keep slipping it out of my field of vision, which forced me to strain, squirm and nudge her to bring the book closer. Naturally, I had barely read the first paragraph when Raisa Nikitovna began to quiz the class. To my horror, one question was directed at me. As I began to answer in my halting Russian, all the children turned to stare at me.

When the lesson was finished, Raisa Nikitovna introduced me to the class. 'This is Esther Rudomin, who comes from Poland. As you can tell, she does not know Russian well and she will have to work hard to catch up. She will share her books with Svetlana. Stand up Svetlana.' Svetlana turned out to be the pretty little girl sitting next to me; the prospect of sharing with her was not heartening[2]. The more attention I got in class, the more she sulked. I sensed that Svetlana wanted to be the queen bee and that I had become her natural enemy. This was confirmed when I asked if I might come to her house and study with her. The answer was a sharp 'No!' I would be allowed to go there to fetch books but when she had finished with them, but otherwise I could jolly well trot home and study alone.

At the end of my first day at school, I went home and collapsed onto the sofa. Out of the confusion of the day, three giants emerged to be slain[3]: Svetlana, Raisa Nikitovna and the Russian alphabet.

---

1 grudgingly = unwillingly

2 heartening = comforting

3 slain = in this context: conquered

Foundation and Paper 1 (Reading): Practice Papers

Section A

Read the passage from *The Endless Steppe* by Esther Hautzig.

Then, select the correct answer for each multiple-choice question.

For question 5, provide a short answer in full sentences.

Re-read lines 1–13.

1. On the day Esther is to go to her new school, she wakes up 'in a blackness as mysterious as the heart of a dark forest'. (lines 1–2) This means:

    a) she wakes up in the middle of a gloomy wood

    b) she wakes in a magical land

    c) she wakes in a strange darkness

    d) she wakes in the shadows at the edge of woodland. (1)

2. Which of these statements is TRUE?

    a) Esther is well-prepared for her new Russian school, with possessions and clothes.

    b) Esther has enough equipment but unsuitable clothes.

    c) Esther has little equipment but warm clothes.

    d) Esther has neither suitable equipment nor clothes. (2)

3. How does Esther feel as she walks to school?

    a) She is unconcerned at walking alone, along an empty road, but anxious about the lessons ahead.

    b) She is afraid she looks like a stranger, without her mother by her side.

    c) She is proud to be starting school alone, brave to be walking along a deserted Siberian road.

    d) She wishes she was at the bakery with her mother, rather than out in the cold. (2)

Re-read lines 14–24.

4. Raisa Nikitovna, Esther's new teacher, is:

    a) welcoming and understanding

    b) unwelcoming and blunt

    c) fierce but friendly

    d) surprised at Esther's arrival and irritated by the unexpected event. (2)

5. As the lesson begins, everyone has a book but Esther. 'The feeling must have been something like a soldier without a gun.' (line 21) What does this mean? (2)

Re-read lines 25–31.

6. Which of the following statements best summarises Esther's memory that her first lesson is a 'chilly one'?

    a) Esther could not read the Russian letters or words and her coat was thin.

    b) Esther could not understand the book, nor could she see it and her chair was uncomfortable.

    c) Esther could not understand the letters, had to struggle to see the book and was unable to read a paragraph.

    d) The letters were strange, Esther's neighbour hardly shared the book and the teacher asked her a question. (2)

Foundation: Practice Paper 1: *The Endless Steppe*

7 'I sensed that Svetlana wanted to be the queen bee and that I had become her natural enemy.' (line 37)

This sentence contains:

   a) a simile and no connective

   b) personification and a simile

   c) a metaphor and a connective

   d) two examples of personification. (2)

8 Which of the following statements is FALSE?

   a) Esther is brave and determined on her first day.

   b) Esther is given a warm welcome by her teacher and her class mate.

   c) Esther is exhausted from all that the first day entails.

   d) Esther is expected at the school but receives a cold reception. (2)

(Total marks for this section: 15)

Section B

Answer the following questions in full sentences.

Re-read lines 1–16.

9 What does the author reveal about Esther's recent move and home life?

Refer to three details in your answer. (3)

10 Esther later realises she must have looked like a stranger as she walked to school.

Why is this? Explain your answer with details from the text. (4)

Re-read lines 17–43.

11 Explain what you think the teacher, Raisa Nikitovna, might feel towards:

   a) Esther (3)

   b) Svetlana. (3)

12 At the end of the day, Esther felt 'three giants emerged to be slain' (line 42):

- Svetlana
- Raisa Nikitovna
- the Russian alphabet

Explain why these were 'giants' to Esther and briefly explain how each might be 'slain'. (6)

13 What are your impressions of Esther:

   a) as she walks to school? (3)

   b) in dealing with her first day? (3)

(Total marks for this section: 25)

Foundation and Paper 1 (Reading): Practice Papers

Section C

14 Imagine Svetlana writes a diary that evening. Write the entry.

You should explore:
- Svetlana's observations about Esther
- her feelings about her
- her thoughts about working together with Esther in the future. (10)

(Total marks for this section: 10)

(Total marks for paper: 50)

Foundation: Practice Paper 2

From *The Girl with a Pearl Earring* by Tracy Chevalier (1999)

> This extract is from near the beginning of the novel, set in Holland in 1664. Griet describes the morning when she meets an artist and his wife for the first time, for whom she will work as a servant.

My mother appeared in the doorway, her eyes two warnings. Behind her the woman had to duck her head because she was so tall, taller than the man following her.

All of our family, even my father and brother, were small.

The woman looked as if she had been blown about by the wind, although it was a calm day. Her cap was askew[1] so that tiny blond curls escaped and hung about her forehead like bees which she swatted at impatiently several times. Her collar needed straightening and was not as crisp as it could be. She pushed her grey mantle[2] back from her shoulders, and I saw then that under her dark blue dress a baby was growing. It would arrive by the year's end, or before.

The woman's face was like an oval serving plate, flashing at times, dull at others. Her eyes were two light brown buttons, a colour I had rarely seen coupled with blond hair. She made a show of watching me hard, but could not fix her attention on me, her eyes darting about the room.

'This is the girl, then,' she said abruptly.

'This is my daughter, Griet,' my mother replied. I nodded respectfully to the man and woman.

'Well. She's not very big. Is she strong enough?' As the woman turned to look at the man, a fold of her mantle caught the handle of the knife I had been using, knocking it off the table so that it spun across the floor.

The woman cried out.

'Catharina,' the man said calmly. He spoke her name as if he held cinnamon[3] in his mouth. The woman stopped, making an effort to quiet herself.

I stepped over and picked up the knife, polishing the blade on my apron before placing it back on the table. The knife had brushed against the vegetables. I set a piece of carrot back in its place.

The man was watching me, his eyes grey like the sea. He had a long, angular face, and his expression was steady, in contrast to his wife's, which flickered like a candle. He had no beard or moustache, and I was glad, for it gave him a clean appearance. He wore a black cloak over his shoulders, a white shirt, and a fine lace collar. His hat pressed into hair the red of brick washed by rain.

'What have you been doing here, Griet?' he asked.

I was surprised by the question but knew enough to hide it. 'Chopping vegetables, sir. For the soup.'

I always laid vegetables out in a circle, each with its own section like a slice of pie. There were five slices: red cabbage, onions, leeks, carrots, and turnips. I had used a knife edge to shape each slice, and placed a carrot disc in the centre.

The man tapped his finger on the table. 'Are they laid out in the order in which they will go into the soup?' he suggested, studying the circle.

'No, sir.' I hesitated. I could not say why I had laid out the vegetables as I did. I simply set them as I felt they should be, but I was too frightened to say so to a gentleman.

---

[1] askew = at an angle

[2] mantle = a long heavy cloak

[3] cinnamon = a strong-smelling spice

'I see you have separated the whites,' he said, indicating the turnips and onions. 'And then the orange and the purple, they do not sit together. Why is that?' He picked up a shred of cabbage and a piece of carrot and shook them like dice in his hand.

I looked at my mother, who nodded slightly.

'The colours fight when they are side by side, sir.'

He arched his eyebrows, as if he had not expected such a response. 'And do you spend much time setting out the vegetables before you make the soup?'

'Oh no, sir,' I replied, confused. I did not want him to think I was idle.

From the corner of my eye I saw a movement. My sister, Agnes, was peering round the doorpost and had shaken her head at my response. I did not often lie. I looked down.

Foundation: Practice Paper 2: *The Girl with a Pearl Earring*

Section A

Read the passage from *The Girl with a Pearl Earring* by Tracy Chevalier.

Then, select the correct answer for each multiple-choice question.

For question 3, provide a short answer in full sentences.

Re-read the introduction.

1. An artist and his wife come to Griet's house. She will become their:
   a) friend
   b) maid
   c) tutor
   d) companion. (1)

Re-read lines 1–9.

2. Griet's mother's eyes are 'two warnings' (line 1). This is:
   a) a simile – to warn the visitors to be kind
   b) a simile – to warn Griet to be on her best behaviour
   c) a metaphor – to warn Griet to be on her best behaviour
   d) a metaphor – to warn the visitors to be kind. (2)

3. Why do you think that Griet compares the height of the woman to the height of her own family (lines 2–3)? (2)

4. 'Her cap was askew' (line 5). What does 'askew' mean in this context?
   a) Her cap has decorative holes in it.
   b) Her cap is square-shaped.
   c) Her cap is too small for her.
   d) Her cap is placed crookedly on her head. (2)

Re-read line 20.

5. This short sentence is in a paragraph of its own. Which statement best explains why it is written like this?
   a) The author cannot think of anything else to say at this point.
   b) The author wants to use simple language.
   c) It is a moment of tense drama and the author wants it to stand out.
   d) It creates a tense atmosphere. (2)

Re-read lines 37–40.

6. Griet replies 'No, sir.' to the man's question. Why do you think her reply is so short?
   a) She sees the woman glaring at her and so is brief.
   b) She does not know how to answer his question and is nervous of him.
   c) She does not really understand the question.
   d) She cannot say much as the onions are making her eyes water. (2)

Foundation and Paper 1 (Reading): Practice Papers

Re-read lines 41–47.

7 Why do you think he 'arched his eyebrows' at her next reply? (line 46)

    a) Her answer surprises and interests him.

    b) He is stretching his face muscles.

    c) He is thinking about something else.

    d) He thinks her reply is funny. (2)

8 Which of these best sums up what we know of Griet?

    a) She is observant and respectful.

    b) She is honest and talkative.

    c) She is dishonest and rude.

    d) She is strange and untidy. (2)

(Total marks for this section: 15)

Section B

Answer the following questions in full sentences.

Re-read lines 4–19.

9 Griet does not particularly like the woman. Explain how each of the following quotations are reasons why she feels this. You do not need to re-write the quotations.

- 'Her collar needed straightening and was not as crisp as it could be.' (lines 6–7)
- 'The woman's face was … flashing at times, dull at others.' (line 10)
- 'She made a show of watching me hard but could not fix her attention on me, her eyes darting about the room'. (lines 11–13)
- 'Well. She's not very big. Is she strong enough?' (line 17)

(8)

Re-read lines 14–16.

10 What do you notice about:

    a) the words the woman uses? (2)

    b) Griet's mother's reply? (2)

Re-read lines 21–32.

11 Consider what the man looks like and what he says.

    Find and write down four quotations which suggest that Griet takes a liking to him. (4)

Re-read lines 31–45.

12 a) Why do you think the man asks Griet several questions about what she is doing with the vegetables? Suggest three reasons. (3)

    b) Griet's answer 'The colours fight when they are side by side, sir.' (line 45) is an example of personification.

    Explain what you think she means here. (2)

Foundation: Practice Paper 2: *The Girl with a Pearl Earring*

Re-read lines 46–50.

13 As far as possible, answer in your own words.

    a) What is the lie? (1)

    b) Why does Griet lie? (1)

    c) Why does she look down? (line 50) (2)

(Total marks for this section: 25)

Section C

14 Griet's mother says little during this extract but she is observing the artist and his wife who may employ her daughter.

    Re-tell the story from her point of view.

    You should explore:

- her observations and reactions to the woman
- her feelings towards Griet
- her thoughts about the man's questions and Griet's replies. (10)

(Total marks for this section: 10)

(Total marks for paper: 50)

Foundation: Practice Paper 3

From *The Adventures of Tom Sawyer* by Mark Twain (1876)

> The story is set in America in the 1840s. In this extract Tom and his friend Huckleberry have a plan to meet after dark, to look for adventure.

[1 perceptible = noticeable]

[2 death-watch = a small beetle which makes a ticking sound, said to warn of death]

[3 melancholy caterwauling = the sorrowful screech of a cat]

[4 oppressive = burdensome, uncomfortable]

At half past nine that night, Tom and Sid were sent to bed as usual. They said their prayers and Sid was soon asleep. Tom lay awake and waited in restless impatience. When it seemed to him that it must be nearly daylight, he heard the clock strike ten! This was despair. He would have tossed and fidgeted, as his nerves demanded, but he was afraid he might wake Sid. So he lay still and stared into the dark. Everything was dismally still. By and by, out of the stillness, little, scarcely perceptible[1] noises began to emphasise themselves. The ticking of the clock began to bring itself into notice. Old beams began to crack mysteriously. The stairs creaked faintly. Evidently spirits were abroad. A measured, muffled snore issued from Aunt Polly's chamber. And now the tiresome chirping of a cricket that no human ingenuity could locate, began. Next the ghastly ticking of a death-watch[2] in the wall at the bed's head made Tom shudder – it meant that somebody's days were numbered. Then the howl of a far-off dog rose on the night air and was answered by a fainter howl from a remoter distance. Tom was in an agony.

At last he was satisfied that time had ceased and eternity begun; he began to doze in spite of himself; the clock chimed eleven, but he did not hear it. And then there came, mingling with his half-formed dreams, a most melancholy caterwauling[3]. The raising of a neighbouring window disturbed him. A cry of 'Scat! You devil!' and the crash of an empty bottle against the back of his aunt's wood-shed brought him wide awake, and a single minute later he was dressed and out of the window and creeping along the roof on all fours. He 'meow'd' with caution once or twice as he went; then jumped to the roof of the wood-shed, and thence to the ground. Huckleberry Finn was there … The boys moved off and disappeared in the gloom. At the end of half an hour they were wading through the tall grass of the graveyard …

… Then they waited in silence for what seemed a long time. The hooting of a distant owl was all the sound that troubled the dead stillness. Tom's reflections grew oppressive[4]. He must force some talk. So he said in a whisper: 'Hucky, do you believe the dead people like it for us to be here?'

Huckleberry whispered: 'I wisht I knowed. It's awful solemn like, ain't it?' …

… 'Say, Hucky, – do you reckon Hoss Williams hears us talking?'

'O'course he does. Least his spirit does.'

Tom, after a pause: 'I wish I'd said *Mister* Williams. But I never meant any harm. Everybody calls him Hoss.' …

… Presently Tom seized his comrade's arm and said: 'Sh!'

'What is it, Tom?' and the two clung together with beating hearts.

'Sh! There 'tis again! Didn't you hear it?'

'I –'

'There! Now you hear it!'

'Lord, Tom, they're coming! They're coming, sure. What'll we do?'

'I dono. Think they'll see us?'

40 'Oh, Tom, they can see in the dark, same as cats. I wish I hadn't come.'

'Oh, don't be afeard. I don't believe they'll bother us. We ain't doing any harm. If we keep perfectly still, maybe they won't notice us at all.'

'I'll try to, Tom, but, Lord! I'm all of a shiver.'

'Listen!'

45 The boys bent their heads together and scarcely breathed. A muffled sound of voices floated up from the far end of the graveyard.

'Look! See there!' whispered Tom. 'What is it?'

'It's devil-fire. Oh, Tom, this is awful.'

Foundation and Paper 1 (Reading): Practice Papers

Section A

Read the passage from *The Adventures of Tom Sawyer* by Mark Twain.

Then, select the correct answer for each multiple-choice question.

For questions 5 and 6, provide a short answer in full sentences.

Re-read lines 1–13.

1 Tom and Sid are sent to bed together. Who do you think Sid is?

    a) Tom's brother, whom he admires.

    b) Tom's brother, who is in on the plan.

    c) Tom's brother, who sleeps in the room next door.

    d) Tom's brother, from whom Tom wants to keep his plan secret. (1)

2 What does 'He would have tossed and fidgeted, as his nerves demanded' (lines 3–4) mean?

    a) Tom was feeling frightened about the night ahead.

    b) Tom was fidgety, as he was impatient to start the adventure.

    c) Sid was annoying Tom, putting his nerves on edge.

    d) Tom forced himself to wriggle around in bed. (2)

3 Tom heard 'the ghastly ticking of a death-watch'. (line 10) What is this sound and what does it mean?

    a) It is a beetle in the wall, its noise predicting someone would die soon.

    b) It is a grandfather clock in the hall, chiming to mark the hour.

    c) It is bed bugs in Tom's bed, rustling around.

    d) It is a night watchman in the graveyard, checking his pocket watch. (2)

Re-read lines 14–23.

4 What time was it when Tom left home?

    a) Ten o'clock

    b) Between ten and eleven o'clock

    c) Shortly after eleven o'clock

    d) Six o'clock in the morning (2)

Re-read from line 24 to the end.

5 'Tom's reflections grew oppressive.' (line 25)

   What does this phrase mean? (2)

6 Re-write the following sentence, putting Huckleberry's spoken words into Standard English:

   'I wisht I knowed. It's awful solemn like, ain't it?' (line 28) (2)

7 Why does the author write Huckleberry's spoken words in this way?

    a) All Americans speak in this way.

    b) The author is illustrating Huckleberry's particular way of speaking.

    c) The author made unintentional errors in his writing.

    d) The author is showing that Huckleberry cannot speak properly because he is very young. (2)

Foundation: Practice Paper 3: *The Adventures of Tom Sawyer*

8 Which of the following statements is TRUE?
   a) Hoss Williams is alive and walking towards them.
   b) Cats can see in the dark and have spotted them.
   c) Real people, carrying flaming torchlights, are coming towards them.
   d) Ghosts are coming out of the mist. (2)

(Total marks for this section: 15)

Section B

Answer the following questions in full sentences.

Re-read lines 1–13.

9 The clock striking or ticking is mentioned three times in these lines.

   Find and write down two such quotations. Each time explain what Tom is doing or thinking. (4)

Re-read lines 5–13.

10 a) Find two quotations that create an eerie atmosphere. (2)
    b) For each quotation explain how the author achieves this. (4)

From lines 1–23:

11 In your own words, suggest three things that make the boys' plan go smoothly without being discovered. (6)

Re-read lines 24–25.

12 Explain how the writer builds tension in each of the following phrases:
    - 'they waited in silence for what seemed a long time'
    - 'The hooting of a distant owl'
    - 'was all the sound that troubled the dead stillness' (6)

Re-read from line 31 to the end.

13 Who is the more afraid, Tom or Huckleberry? Support your answer with evidence from the text. (3)

(Total marks for this section: 25)

Section C

14 Using the information in the text you have read so far, continue the story of Tom and Huckleberry's adventure that night. If you choose to use dialogue, it does not have to follow the style in the extract.

   You should consider:
   - what Tom and Huckleberry see coming towards them
   - how each boy would react to what he sees
   - how their night adventure ends. (10)

(Total marks for this section: 10)

(Total marks for paper: 50)

Paper 1 (Reading): Prose Practice Paper 1

From the memoir *Educated* by Tara Westover (2018)

> The narrator, Tara, and her siblings live with their father. Her grandparents live close by. As part of his religious conviction, Tara's father believes that to drink milk is sinful.

After Dad took up preaching against milk, Grandma jammed her fridge full of it. She and Grandpa only drank skim but pretty soon it was all there – two percent, whole, even chocolate. She seemed to believe this was an important line to hold.

It wasn't long before I began to think of all that milk spoiling in Grandma's fridge. Then I got into the habit of skipping breakfast each morning and going straight to the barn. I'd slop the pigs and fill the troughs for the cows and horses, then I'd hop over the corral fence, loop around the barn and step through Grandma's side door.

On one such morning, as I sat at the counter watching Grandma pour a bowl of cornflakes, she said, 'How would you like to go to school?'

'I wouldn't like it,' I said.

'How do you know,' she barked. 'You ain't never tried it.'

She poured the milk and handed me the bowl, then she perched at the bar, directly across from me, and watched as I shovelled spoonfuls into my mouth.

'We're leaving tomorrow for Arizona,' she told me, but I already knew. She and Grandpa always went to Arizona when the weather began to turn. Grandpa said he was too old for Idaho winters; the cold put an ache in his bones. 'Get yourself up real early,' Grandma said, 'around five, and we'll take you with us. Put you in school.'

I shifted on my stool. I tried to imagine school but couldn't. Instead I pictured Sunday school, which I attended each week and which I hated. A boy named Aaron had told all the girls that I couldn't read because I didn't go to school, and now none of them would talk to me.

'Dad said I can go?' I said.

'No,' Grandma said. 'But we'll be long gone by the time he realizes you're missing.' She sat my bowl in the sink and gazed out the window.

Grandma was a force of nature – impatient, aggressive, self-possessed. To look at her was to take a step back. She dyed her hair black and this intensified her already severe features, especially her eyebrows, which she smeared on each morning in thick, inky arches. She drew them too large and this made her face seem stretched. They were also drawn too high and draped the rest of her features into an expression of boredom, almost sarcasm.

'You should be in school,' she said.

'Won't Dad just make you bring me back?' I said.

'Your dad can't make me do a damned thing.' Grandma stood, squaring herself. 'If he wants you, he'll have to come get you.' She hesitated, and for a moment looked ashamed. 'I talked to him yesterday. He won't be able to fetch you back for a long while. He's behind on that shed he's building in town. He can't pack up and drive to Arizona, not while the weather holds and he and the boys can work long days.'

Paper 1 (Reading): Prose Practice Paper 1: *Educated*

Grandma's scheme was well plotted. Dad always worked from sunup until sundown in the weeks before the first snow, trying to stockpile enough money from hauling scrap and building barns to outlast the winter, when jobs were scarce. Even if his mother ran off with his youngest child, he wouldn't be able to stop working, not until the forklift was encased in ice.

40 'I'll need to feed the animals before we go,' I said. 'He'll notice I'm gone for sure if the cows break through the fence looking for water.'

I didn't sleep that night. I sat on the kitchen floor and watched the hours tick by. One A.M. Two. Three.

Section A

Read the extract from *Educated* by Tara Westover.

Then, select the correct answer for each multiple-choice question.

Re-read the introduction.

1 Where do Tara and her family live?
 a) Tara lives with her grandparents; her father and siblings live close by.
 b) Tara lives with her father; her grandparents and her siblings live close by.
 c) Tara lives with her father and her siblings; her grandparents live close by.
 d) Tara lives with her siblings; her father and grandparents live close by. (1)

Re-read lines 5–7.

'I'd slop the pigs ... through Grandma's side door.'

2 Which statement best describes the use and effect of verbs in this sentence?
 a) The list effect of five short verbs emphasises Tara's speed.
 b) All the verbs make it easy for the reader to understand.
 c) The verbs suggest that it was all hard work for Tara.
 d) The seven verbs indicate that it was long and boring for Tara. (2)

Re-read lines 8–20.

3 Which of the following is TRUE?
 a) This section contains only dialogue and description of actions.
 b) This section contains only description of actions and thoughts.
 c) This section contains only dialogue and thoughts.
 d) This section contains dialogue, description of actions and thoughts. (2)

Re-read lines 24–28.

4 Why does Tara describe her grandmother as 'a force of nature'? (line 24)
 a) because she looks as if she has been blown about by the wind
 b) because she is a small woman who is at the mercy of the elements
 c) because everything about her is calm and natural
 d) because she has a strong and unforgettable personality (2)

5 Which of Tara's grandmother's facial features most particularly affects her overall expression?
 a) her hair
 b) her nose
 c) her eyebrows
 d) her mouth (2)

Paper 1 (Reading): Prose Practice Paper 1: *Educated*

Re-read lines 30–39.

6 'Grandma stood, squaring herself.' (line 31) What does this mean?
   a) that she turned away from Tara and looked strict
   b) that she adjusted her clothing carefully as she was feeling anxious
   c) that she stood firm and looked determined
   d) that she lowered her shoulders as she was feeling nervous (2)

7 Why is Grandma's scheme 'well plotted'? (line 36)
   a) because Tara's father is happy that she goes away to school
   b) because Tara's father has to keep working while the weather is good
   c) because Tara's father does not have a car to collect her with
   d) because Tara's father needs to stay at home with her siblings (2)

8 This text is:
   a) autobiographical and written in the first person
   b) a biography and written in the third person
   c) a biography and written in the first person
   d) autobiographical and written in the third person. (2)

(Total marks for this section: 15)

Section B
Answer the following questions in full sentences.

Re-read lines 1–7.

9 a) Why does Grandma have so much milk in her fridge? (2)
   b) Why do you think Tara goes to her grandmother's house every morning? (2)

Re-read lines 8–24.

10 Look at the sequence of events here. Why is Tara unable to offer much resistance to her grandmother's scheme to take her to Arizona? (5)

Re-read lines 42–43.

11 a) How is Tara's inability to sleep that night emphasised? (4)
   b) Suggest reasons for her inability to sleep. Support each reason with close reference to the text. (6)

12 Looking at the text as a whole, what qualities does Tara possess? Support your points with evidence from the text. (6)

(Total marks for this section: 25)

Foundation and Paper 1 (Reading): Practice Papers

Section C

13 How does the author and narrator, Tara Westover, present the character of her grandmother?

Develop three points of argument, each in a separate paragraph.

In your answer, you should explore:

- the relationship between Tara's grandmother and father
- her physical appearance and what this suggests
- the nature of the conversation she has with Tara.

Support each point with evidence; explain how the evidence helps to present the character of the grandmother. (10)

(Total marks for this section: 10)

(Total marks for paper: 50)

Paper 1 (Reading): Prose Practice Paper 2

From *Reckless* by Cornelia Funke (2010)

This extract is from the first edition of *Reckless*, which was later re-written and published as *Reckless 1: The Petrified Flesh*.

12-year-old Jacob is desperate to find his father, John Reckless, who has disappeared.

The night breathed through the apartment like a dark animal. The ticking of a clock. The groan of a floorboard as he slipped out of his room. All was drowned by its silence. But Jacob loved the night. He felt it on his skin like a promise. Like a cloak woven from freedom and danger.

5   Outside the stars were paled by the glaring lights of the city, and the large apartment was stale with his mother's sorrow. She did not wake as Jacob stole into her room, even when he carefully opened the drawer of her bedside table. The key lay right next to the pills that let her sleep. Its cool metal nestled in his hand as he stepped back out into the dark corridor.

10 There was a light burning in his brother's room – Will was afraid of the dark – and Jacob made sure he was fast asleep before unlocking the door to their father's study. Their mother had not entered there since his disappearance, but for Jacob this was not the first time he had sneaked into the empty room to search for the answers she did not want to give.

15 It still looked as if John Reckless had last sat in his desk chair less than an hour ago, instead of more than a year. The sweater he had worn so often hung over the chair, and a used tea bag was desiccating on a plate next to his calendar, which still showed the weeks of a previous year.

Come back! Jacob wrote it with his finger on the fogged up window, on the dusty desk, and
20 on the glass panels of the cabinet that still held the old pistols his father had collected. But the room remained silent – and empty. He was twelve and no longer had a father. Jacob kicked at the drawers he had searched in vain for so many nights. In a silent rage, he yanked the books and magazines from the shelves, tore down the model aeroplanes that hung above the desk, ashamed at how proud he had once been when his father had allowed him to paint
25 one with red varnish.

Come back! He wanted to scream it through the streets that cut their gleaming path through the city blocks seven storeys below, scream it at the thousand windows that punched squares of light into the night.

The sheet of paper slipped out of a book on aircraft propulsion. Jacob only picked it up
30 because he thought he recognised his father's handwriting on it, though he quickly realised his error. Symbols and equations, a sketch of a peacock, a sun, two moons. None of it made any sense. Except for the one sentence he read on the reverse side:

THE MIRROR WILL OPEN ONLY FOR HE WHO CANNOT SEE HIMSELF

Jacob turned around – and his glance was met by his own reflection.

35 The mirror. He still remembered very well the day his father had mounted it on the wall. It hung between the shelves like a shimmering eye, a glassy abyss that cast back a warped reflection on everything John Reckless had left behind: his desk, the old pistols, his books – and his elder son.

40 The glass was so uneven one could barely recognise one's own reflection, and it was darker than other mirrors, but the rose tendrils winding across the silver frame looked so real they seemed ready to wilt at any moment.

THE MIRROR WILL OPEN ONLY FOR HE WHO CANNOT SEE HIMSELF

Jacob closed his eyes.

Paper 1 (Reading): Prose Practice Paper 2: *Reckless*

Section A

Read the extract from *Reckless* by Cornelia Funke.

Then, select the correct answer for each multiple-choice question.

For question 8, provide a short answer in a full sentence.

Re-read lines 1–14.

1. The extract is written:
   a) in the first person, about Jacob, who lives with his father and mother
   b) in the second person, about Will, who lives with his mother and brother
   c) in the third person, about Jacob, who lives with his mother and brother
   d) in the first person, about John Reckless and his family. (1)

2. Why does Jacob love the night?
   a) He loves the quiet, when everyone else is asleep, and to wear his special woven cloak.
   b) He feels he has an agreement with the night that brings freedom and danger. He is not afraid of the freedom and danger it might bring.
   c) He feels promises will come true and he is exposed to exciting adventures.
   d) There is a deep silence and wild animals come alive in his dreams. (2)

Re-read lines 5–6.

3. 'Outside the stars were paled by the glaring lights of the city, and the large apartment was stale with his mother's sorrow.' This sentence contains:
   a) a compound sentence with an abstract noun
   b) a simple sentence with three adjectives
   c) a complex sentence with a subordinate clause and six nouns
   d) a simple sentence with two verbs. (2)

4. Unlike Jacob, why do his mother and brother not like the night-time?
   a) Jacob's mother cries about her husband; this keeps his brother, Will, awake.
   b) Jacob's mother stays awake guarding the key to her husband's study; Will misses his father.
   c) Jacob's mother cannot sleep, so takes sleeping pills; Will is fearful of the dark.
   d) Jacob's mother lies awake in sorrow; Will needs the light on in the corridor. (2)

Re-read lines 15–25.

5. Which of the following statements best describes John Reckless?
   a) A man who did not look after his possessions and left clothing and tea bags lying around.
   b) A man who enjoyed working and reading books and magazines, but not much else.
   c) A man whose only interests were in guns and weaponry.
   d) A well-read man, with interests in planes and guns, who painted models with Jacob. (2)

29

Foundation and Paper 1 (Reading): Practice Papers

Re-read lines 29–43.

6 Jacob finds a strange note:

   a) which fell out of a book on planes, with symbols and pictures on the front and one sentence on the back

   b) which fell from a model plane propeller that had his father's handwriting on one side

   c) which fell out of a book on planes, and had just one mysterious sentence written on the back

   d) which was between books on the shelf and had symbols and diagrams on both sides. (2)

7 The mirror is described 'like a shimmering eye, a glassy abyss'. (line 36) What does this mean?

   a) The mirror sparkled, like an eye, as its front was made of a special type of glass.

   b) The mirror was in the shape of an eye with a glazed finish to it, taken from an abbey.

   c) The mirror seemed to twinkle, as if with a black rock behind it.

   d) The mirror seemed to be watching, with a great dark hole beyond its glass front. (2)

8 THE MIRROR WILL OPEN ONLY FOR HE WHO CANNOT SEE HIMSELF

   Write the meaning of the riddle in your own words. (2)

(Total marks for this section: 15)

Section B

Answer the following questions in full sentences.

9 Look again at line 1.

   'The night breathed through the apartment like a dark animal.'

   a) What atmosphere is introduced? (1)

   b) How does the author create this atmosphere? (4)

10 '*Come back!*' (line 19 and line 26) is written in italics.

   Why do you think this is? (3)

Re-read lines 15–28.

11 Was John Reckless' disappearance a sudden one?

   Support your view with quotations. (4)

Re-read lines 26–28.

12 How is Jacob feeling? How does the author use imagery to show this? (5)

13 Look at the passage as a whole.

   What are your impressions of:

   a) Jacob's mother? (4)

   b) Jacob's father, John Reckless? (4)

   Support your ideas with details from the text.

(Total marks for this section: 25)

Paper 1 (Reading): Prose Practice Paper 2: *Reckless*

Section C

14 How does the author, Cornelia Funke, use the senses to create and build a sense of mystery for the reader?

Develop three points of argument, each in a separate paragraph.

In your answer, you should explore the ways in which she describes:

- the use of sounds within the apartment as Jacob moves around
- the use of touch in his father's study
- the use of sight in his description of the mirror.

Support each point with evidence; explain how the author creates and builds mystery for the reader. (10)

(Total marks for this section: 10)

(Total marks for paper: 50)

Paper 1 (Reading): Prose Practice Paper 3

From *The Shadow of the Wind* by Carlos Ruiz Zafón (2001)

> The story is set in Barcelona, Spain, in 1945. Daniel and his father are visiting the 'Cemetery of Forgotten Books' together for the first time.

Night watchmen still lingered in the misty streets when we stepped out of the front door. The lamps along the Ramblas marked out an avenue in the early morning haze as the city awoke, like a watercolour slowly coming to life. When we reached Calle Arco del Teatro, we continued through its arch towards the Raval quarter, entering a vault of blue haze. I followed my father through that narrow lane, more of a scar than a street, until the glimmer of the Ramblas faded behind us. The brightness of dawn filtered down from balconies and cornices[1] in streaks of slanting light that dissolved before touching the ground. At last my father stopped in front of a large door of carved wood, blackened by time and humidity. Before us loomed what to my eyes seemed the carcass of a palace, a place of echoes and shadows.

'Daniel, you mustn't tell anyone what you're about to see today. Not even your friend Tomas. No one.'

A smallish man with vulturine features framed by thick grey hair opened the door. His impenetrable aquiline[2] gaze rested on mine.

'Good morning, Isaac. This is my son, Daniel,' my father announced. 'He'll be eleven soon, and one day the shop will be his. It's time he knew this place.'

The man called Isaac nodded and invited us in. A blue-tinted gloom obscured the sinuous contours of a marble staircase and a gallery of frescoes peopled with angels and fabulous creatures. We followed our host through a palatial corridor and arrived at a sprawling round hall where a spiralling basilica[3] of shadows was pierced by shafts of light from a high glass dome above us. A labyrinth of passageways and crammed bookshelves rose from base to pinnacle like a beehive, woven with tunnels, steps, platforms and bridges that presaged[4] an immense library of seemingly impossible geometry. I looked at my father, stunned. He smiled at me and winked.

'Welcome to the Cemetery of Forgotten Books, Daniel.'

Scattered among the library's corridors and platforms I could make out about a dozen human figures. Some of them turned to greet me from afar, and I recognised the faces of various colleagues of my father's, fellows of the secondhand booksellers' guild. To my ten-year-old eyes, they looked like a brotherhood of alchemists in furtive study. My father knelt next to me and, with his eyes fixed on mine, addressed me in the hushed voice he reserved for promises and secrets.

'This is a place of mystery, Daniel, a sanctuary. Every book, every volume you see here, has a soul. The soul of the person who wrote it and of those who read it and lived and dreamed with it. Every time a book changes hands, every time someone runs his eyes down its pages, its spirit grows and strengthens. This place was already ancient when my father brought me here for the first time, many years ago. Perhaps as old as the city itself. Nobody knows for certain how long it has existed, or who created it. I will tell you what my father told me, though. When a library disappears, or a bookshop closes down, when a book is consigned to oblivion, those of us who know this place, its guardians, make sure that it gets here. In this place, books no longer remembered by anyone, books that are lost in time, live for ever, waiting for the day when they will reach a new reader's hands. In the shop we buy and sell them, but in truth books have no owner. Every book you see here has been someone else's best friend. Now they only have us, Daniel. Do you think you'll be able to keep such a secret?'

My gaze was lost in the immensity of the place and its sorcery of light. I nodded, and my father smiled.

---

[1] cornices = ornamental moulding just below the ceiling

[2] aquiline = like an eagle

[3] basilica = large dome

[4] presaged = pointed to/introduced

Paper 1 (Reading): Prose Practice Paper 3: *The Shadow of the Wind*

Section A

Read the passage from *The Shadow of the Wind* by Carlos Ruiz Zafón.

Then, select the correct answer for each multiple-choice question.

For question 3, provide a short answer in a full sentence.

Re-read lines 1–16.

1. Which statement best explains Daniel's first impression of the Cemetery of Forgotten Books as a 'carcass of a palace, a place of echoes and shadows'? (lines 9–10)

    a) a palace full of sound and light with a feeling of happiness

    b) a fine building but decayed with a sense of mystery

    c) a building with a fine structure with a feeling of adventure

    d) an historic old fort with a history of hidden secrets (1)

2. Why was this an important day for Daniel?

    a) He will be eleven soon and this is a special outing with his father to revisit the Cemetery of Forgotten Books.

    b) He is 10 years old, and his father is taking him to the secondhand bookshop, where he works.

    c) He is 12 years old and is visiting the Cemetery of Forgotten Books for the first time as one day he will take it over.

    d) He will be 11 years old soon and is visiting the Cemetery of Forgotten Books for the first time as he will one day inherit his father's bookshop. (2)

3. Re-write the father's words in lines 11–12 as indirect speech. (2)

Re-read lines 17–23.

4. Which of the following statements describing the inside of the building is FALSE?

    a) There was a marble winding staircase with paintings of angels and magnificent animals.

    b) A grand passageway led to a circular hall with a glass roof at the top casting shadows.

    c) Corridors of bookshelves joined by tunnels and stages descended steeply.

    d) Shelves packed with books ran along corridors arranged in a complex hive formation to the top. (2)

5. What are the effects of the sentence structures in this paragraph?

    a) Long and short sentences are interwoven to engage the reader and maintain pace in the description.

    b) Long sentences slow the pace to allow for detailed description, followed by short sentences emphasising what has gone before.

    c) Long sentences show it was a big building to walk around, followed by short sentences for relief when the walk was over.

    d) Long sentences show time is dragging for Daniel; short sentences are a snappy ending to the paragraph. (2)

Foundation and Paper 1 (Reading): Practice Papers

Re-read lines 31–34.

6 What does the word 'guardians' (line 38) mean in this context?

    a) workers who care for the building and are custodians of old books

    b) workers who act as guards and caretakers for the ancient building

    c) workers who are guardian angels, spirits, who care for the soul of books

    d) workers who are owners of the books and take care with their repair   (2)

7 Daniel's father is the only one to speak. Why is this?

    a) Daniel is only 10 and an unimportant figure and his voice would add nothing to the text.

    b) The text is written from Daniel's father's point of view, and so it is his voice we hear.

    c) Daniel's father is the central figure showing Daniel a new world; Daniel is too amazed to speak.

    d) Daniel's father's gaze discourages both Daniel and Isaac from making conversation.   (2)

8 What tone is set in the final two lines?

    a) Disbelief and amazement: Daniel cannot believe all he has seen and is reluctant to keep the secret.

    b) Magic and mystery: Daniel is enchanted by all he sees and agrees to continue to keep the secret.

    c) Witchcraft and horror: Daniel is stunned by all he sees and too afraid not to keep the secret.

    d) Suspicion and unease: Daniel cannot understand all he has seen; it must be trickery of the light.   (2)

(Total marks for this section: 15)

Section B

Answer the following questions in full sentences.

Re-read lines 1–7.

9 a) Choose two quotations from the description of the city that morning that you find vivid and effective.   (2)

    b) Explain your choices.   (4)

Re-read lines 13–14.

10 Describe Isaac in your own words, as far as possible.   (3)

Re-read lines 26–28.

11 Daniel thinks people working there look 'like a brotherhood of alchemists in furtive study'.

   Explain what he means.   (4)

12 What sort of a person is Daniel's father?

   Use evidence from the whole passage in your answer.   (6)

Re-read lines 31–42.

13 Do you think Daniel's father's belief in the life of a book is a valid one?

   With reference to the text, to what extent do you agree?   (6)

(Total marks for this section: 25)

Paper 1 (Reading): Prose Practice Paper 3: *The Shadow of the Wind*

Section C

14 How does the author, Carlos Ruiz Zafón, use language within Daniel's narrative perspective to present the impact of the 'Cemetery of Forgotten Books' on Daniel?

Develop three points of argument, each in a separate paragraph.

In your answer, you should explore the ways in which he describes:

- how Daniel describes and explains the inside of the building
- how Daniel reacts to the building and its people
- how Daniel's father speaks to him.

Support each point with evidence; explain how the evidence demonstrates the impact of the 'Cemetery of Forgotten Books' on Daniel. (10)

(Total marks for this section: 10)

(Total marks for paper: 50)

Paper 1 (Reading): Poetry Practice Paper 1

'The Choosing' by Liz Lochhead (1972)

We were first equal Mary and I
with same coloured ribbons in mouse-coloured hair
and with equal shyness,
we curtseyed to the lady councillor
5   for copies of Collins' Children's Classics.
First equal, equally proud.

Best friends too Mary and I
a common bond in being cleverest (equal)
in our small school's small class.
10 I remember
the competition for top desk
or to read aloud the lesson
at school service.
And my terrible fear
15 of her superiority at sums.

I remember the housing scheme
where we both stayed.
The same houses, different homes,
where the choices were made.

20 I don't know exactly why they moved,
but anyway they went.
Something about a three-apartment
and a cheaper rent.
But from the top deck of the high-school bus
25 I'd glimpse among the others on the corner
Mary's father, mufflered[1], contrasting strangely
with the elegant greyhounds[2] by his side.
He didn't believe in high school education,
especially for girls,
30 or in forking out for uniforms.

[1] mufflered = wearing a scarf around the neck for warmth

[2] greyhounds = greyhound racing is an organised, competitive sport in which greyhounds are raced around a track. Greyhound races often allow the public to bet on the outcome.

Ten years later on a Saturday –
I am coming home from the library –
sitting near me on the bus,
Mary
35 with a husband who is tall,
curly haired, has eyes
for no one else but Mary.
Her arms are round the full-shaped vase
that is her body.
40 Oh, you can see where the attraction lies
in Mary's life –
not that I envy her, really.

And I am coming from the library
with my arms full of books.
45 I think of those prizes that were ours for the taking
and wonder when the choices got made
we don't remember making.

Foundation and Paper 1 (Reading): Practice Papers

Section A

Read the poem 'The Choosing' by Liz Lochhead.

Then, select the correct answer for each multiple-choice question.

Re-read lines 1–9.

1. The main reason for the friendship between the girls is because:
   a) they both wear the same coloured hair ribbons
   b) they are both at the top of the class
   c) they both receive the same book prize
   d) they both feel shy when they collect their prize. (1)

Re-read line 8.

2. Why is '(equal)' in brackets?
   a) because the poet wasn't sure whether to include the word again as it has been used so often
   b) because the brackets around the word are a typing error
   c) because the reader is being humorously reminded, through repetition, that the girls are equal in everything
   d) because it is an afterthought and an unimportant word in the line (2)

Re-read lines 10–15.

3. What is the significance of these lines?
   a) The reader is given further details about Mary's memories of school life.
   b) Mary remembers always being the best at everything, especially sums.
   c) The girls did everything together happily and were not at all competitive with each other.
   d) Competition between the girls is mentioned for the first time which caused the narrator anxiety. (2)

Re-read lines 20–30.

4. Which of these statements best describes Mary's circumstances?
   a) Mary moved house, her father was a little scruffy and he paid for Mary's school uniform.
   b) Mary moved to a cheaper apartment, her father kept greyhounds and he did not want Mary to continue at school.
   c) Mary moved to a different apartment, her father raced greyhounds for money and he did not want to buy Mary's school uniform.
   d) Mary moved to a larger apartment, her father wore a woolly scarf and he wanted Mary to go to high school. (2)

Paper 1 (Reading): Poetry Practice Paper 1: 'The Choosing'

Re-read lines 31–32 and 43–44.

5 What can be assumed from these lines?
   a) The narrator is about 18 years old and works as a librarian on Saturdays.
   b) The narrator is about 30 years old and is employed at the library at the weekend.
   c) The narrator is about 18 years old and studies in the library on a Saturday.
   d) The narrator is about 15 years old and has a weekend job sorting books at the library. (2)

Re-read lines 31–42.

6 Which statement best explains the trigger that prompts the telling of the story?
   a) The narrator sees her old friend Mary, who is now expecting a baby and with a partner.
   b) The narrator sees her old friend Mary on the same bus and wants to speak to her.
   c) The narrator sees her old friend Mary on the bus and hopes that she is not recognised.
   d) The narrator sees her old friend Mary and remembers trying to be as good as her at maths. (2)

Re-read lines 40–42.

7 Which of these statements is FALSE?
   a) The narrator does not envy Mary's life.
   b) The narrator definitely envies Mary's life.
   c) The narrator neither envies nor dislikes Mary's life.
   d) The narrator is unsure of her feelings about Mary's life. (2)

Look again at the title of the poem, and lines 19 and 46.

8 Why do you think the poem is called 'The Choosing' rather than 'The Choices'?
   a) because she does not want to keep repeating the word 'choices'
   b) because she prefers the sound of 'choosing'
   c) because the poem is about who chooses rather than the choices
   d) because it is more original and slightly mysterious (2)

(Total marks for this section: 15)

Section B

Answer the following questions in full sentences.

Re-read lines 1–9.

9 a) Explain the ways in which the narrator and Mary are similar at this stage of their lives. (3)
   b) How is their similarity and friendship emphasised by the poet? (4)

Re-read lines 16–19.

10 Explain how this stanza can be seen as a turning point:
   a) in the girls' lives (2)
   b) because of how it is written. (4)

Foundation and Paper 1 (Reading): Practice Papers

Re-read lines 20–30.

11 a) Why are these observations and details about Mary's house move and father significant to the story? (4)

   b) From these lines, what is learnt about the character of the narrator? (4)

Re-read lines 31–44.

12 Picture this scene on the bus.

   How does the poet emphasise the difference between the two girls' lives? (4)

(Total marks for this section: 25)

Section C

13 How does the structure of the poem aid the reader's understanding of its meaning?

   Develop three points of argument, each in a separate paragraph.

   In your answer, you should explore:

   - the use of stanzas and their changes in focus
   - the use of tense change
   - the use of rhyme and non-rhyme.

   Support each point with evidence and/or explanations; explain how these help your understanding of the meaning of the poem. (10)

(Total marks for this section: 10)

(Total marks for paper: 50)

Paper 1 (Reading): Poetry Practice Paper 2

From 'Sir Gawain and the Green Knight' translated by Simon Armitage (2008)

> 'Sir Gawain and the Green Knight' is a poem about Sir Gawain who accepts a challenge from a mysterious Green Knight. In this extract, the day has arrived for Sir Gawain to seek out the knight.

Now night passes and New Year draws near,
drawing off darkness as our deity decrees.
But wild-looking weather was about in the world:
clouds decanted their cold rain earthwards;
5   the nithering[1] north needled man's very nature;
creatures were scattered by the stinging sleet.
Then a whip-cracking wind comes whistling between hills
driving snow into deepening drifts in the dales.
Alert and listening, Gawain lies in his bed;
10 his lids are lowered but he sleeps very little
as each crow of the cock brings his destiny closer.
Before day had dawned he was up and dressed
for the room was livened by the light of a lamp
To suit him in his metal and to saddle his mount
15 he called for a servant, who came quickly,
bounded from his bedsheets, bringing his garments.
He swathes Sir Gawain in glorious style,
first fastening clothes to fend off the frost,
then his armour, looked after all the while by the household:
20 the buffed and burnished[2] stomach and breastplates,
and the rings of chain-mail, raked free of rust,
all gleaming good as new, for which he is grateful
          indeed.
     With every polished piece
25   no man shone more,
     from here to ancient Greece.
     He sent then for his steed.

[1] nithering = pinching with cold

[2] burnished = polished by rubbing (especially of metal)

Foundation and Paper 1 (Reading): Practice Papers

Section A

Read the extract from 'Sir Gawain and the Green Knight' translated by Simon Armitage.

Then, select the correct answer from each multiple-choice question.

Re-read lines 1–2.

1. What date and time of day is it?
   a) January 1st, midnight
   b) December 31st, afternoon
   c) January 1st, dawn
   d) December 31st, dusk (2)

2. What does 'drawing off darkness ...' (line 2) mean?
   a) There are drawings in the night sky.
   b) Darkness leaves the sky as morning comes.
   c) The sky turns dark black in the morning.
   d) Storm clouds gather at night. (2)

Re-read lines 3–8.

3. The setting that surrounds where Sir Gawain is sleeping is described as:
   a) amongst hills and valleys, with windy weather, heavy rain and snow
   b) in a town in the north of England, with rain and wind
   c) near the sea, with wild weather, whipping up high waves
   d) near the North Pole, with fierce winds, thick snow, ice and sleet. (2)

4. '. . . as each crow of the cock brings his destiny closer.' (line 11)
   This line is important as:
   a) The cock's crow has kept him awake all night; he has slept very little and is unprepared.
   b) Each crow of the cock is a sign of morning; a time he will return to the safety of home.
   c) The cock's crow signals the new day; the day when he is to set off on his challenge and his future will be decided.
   d) Each crow of the cock affects his sleep; he dreams of what bad things may lie ahead. (2)

Re-read lines 14–19.

5. What is learnt of Sir Gawain's servant?
   a) He sadly bathes Sir Gawain and dresses him in his clothes, dreading the day ahead.
   b) He carefully dresses Sir Gawain in armour which he himself has polished and maintained.
   c) He is a reluctant worker, leaving the care of Sir Gawain and his needs to the staff of the house.
   d) He readily brings Sir Gawain's armour, fits him in it and will help saddle his horse. (2)

Paper 1 (Reading): Poetry Practice Paper 2: 'Sir Gawain and the Green Knight'

6 The use of a colon at the end of line 19 is:
   a) to avoid using a conjunction
   b) to introduce a list
   c) to separate two clauses
   d) instead of a full stop. (1)

Re-read lines 24–27.

7 These four lines contain:
   a) one proper noun and three common nouns
   b) one present tense verb and one past tense verb
   c) two present tense verbs
   d) two proper nouns and two common nouns. (2)

8 The day has arrived for Sir Gawain to set off to find the Green Knight.
   Which of the following statements best describes his changing mood?
   a) Sir Gawain feels happy and alert.
   b) Sir Gawain feels worried and weak.
   c) Sir Gawain feels anxious but ready.
   d) Sir Gawain feels foolish but confident. (2)

(Total marks for this section: 15)

Section B

Answer the following questions in full sentences.

Re-read lines 3–8.

9 a) Choose two quotations that describe the 'wild-looking weather' that you find effective. (2)
   b) Explain how these make the description vivid. (4)

Re-read lines 1–13.

10 How does the poet use dark and light to create mood and atmosphere? (6)

Re-read lines 1–22.

11 Hear your voice in your head.
    a) What do you notice about which syllables are stressed? (1)
    b) What is the effect of this technique? (3)

12 What is the function of line 23 in the structure of the extract? (3)

13 Consider the structure and form of the whole extract.
    What changes do you notice between lines 1–22 and 23–27? (6)

(Total marks for this section: 25)

Foundation and Paper 1 (Reading): Practice Papers

Section C

14 How is Sir Gawain's state of mind influenced by events and actions as the day unfolds?

Develop three points of argument, each in a separate paragraph.

In your answer you should explain:
- the events of the weather
- the actions of the servants
- his readiness for action.

Support each point with evidence; explain how the evidence suggests Sir Gawain's state of mind. (10)

(Total marks for this section: 10)

(Total marks for paper: 50)

Paper 1 (Reading): Poetry Practice Paper 3

From 'Snake' by DH Lawrence (1923)

A snake came to my water-trough
On a hot, hot day, and I in pyjamas for the heat,
To drink there.

In the deep, strange-scented shade of the great dark carob tree
5   I came down the steps with my pitcher
And must wait, must stand and wait, for there he was at the trough
    before me.

He reached down from a fissure in the earth-wall in the gloom
And trailed his yellow-brown slackness soft-bellied down, over
10   the edge of the stone trough
And rested his throat upon the stone bottom,
And where the water had dripped from the tap, in a small clearness,
He sipped with his straight mouth,
Softly drank through his straight gums, into his slack long body,
15 Silently.

Someone was before me at my water-trough,
And I, like a second-comer, waiting.

He lifted his head from his drinking, as cattle do,
And looked at me vaguely, as drinking cattle do,
20 And flickered his two-forked tongue from his lips, and mused
        a moment,
And stooped and drank a little more,
Being earth-brown, earth-golden from the burning bowels
    of the earth
25 On the day of Sicilian July, with Etna smoking.

The voice of my education said to me
He must be killed,
For in Sicily the black, black snakes are innocent, the gold
    are venomous.

30 And voices in me said, If you were a man
You would take a stick and break him now, and finish him off.

But must I confess how I liked him,
How glad I was he had come like a guest in quiet, to drink
    at my water-trough
35 And depart peaceful, pacified, and thankless,
Into the burning bowels of this earth?

> Was it cowardice, that I dared not kill him?
> Was it perversity, that I longed to talk to him?
> Was it humility, to feel so honoured?
> 40 I felt so honoured.

Paper 1 (Reading): Poetry Practice Paper 3: From 'Snake'

Section A

Read the extract from 'Snake' by DH Lawrence.

Then, select the correct answer for each multiple-choice question.

Re-read lines 1–15.

1 Why do the poet and the snake both go to the water-trough?
   a) They go there as it is summer.
   b) They are thirsty and go there for water.
   c) They go there because it is morning.
   d) They are hot and want to be in the shade. (1)

2 Which statement most accurately describes where the snake comes from?
   a) from the stone drinking trough
   b) from the gloom
   c) from the great dark carob tree
   d) from a crack in the wall (2)

Re-read lines 16–17.

3 In this context 'Someone was before me …' means:
   a) another person had arrived there first
   b) someone was standing in front of me
   c) the snake had arrived there first
   d) the snake arrived after me. (2)

4 According to the 'voice of my education' (line 26) which snakes should be killed?
   a) black snakes in Sicily
   b) all snakes in Sicily
   c) gold snakes everywhere
   d) gold snakes in Sicily (2)

Re-read line 25.

5 What do you think 'Sicilian July' and 'Etna' refer to?
   a) It is a special day in July and Etna is a river.
   b) It is an unusual month and Etna is the name of the poet's house.
   c) It is July in Sicily and Etna is the name of a volcano.
   d) It is early July and Etna is Sicily's capital city. (2)

Foundation and Paper 1 (Reading): Practice Papers

Re-read lines 37–39.

6   Which statement is FALSE?

    a)   In every line there is a rhetorical question and an abstract noun.

    b)   There is a collective noun in every line.

    c)   Every line begins in the same way.

    d)   In every line there is a verb and a rhetorical question. (2)

Re-read lines 37–40.

7   Why does the poet not kill the snake?

    a)   because he is frightened of it

    b)   because voices in his head tell him not to

    c)   because he feels privileged to see it

    d)   because he thinks the snake is too clever for him (2)

8   Which of these statements best describes the structure of this poem?

    a)   This is a narrative poem written in free verse.

    b)   This is a narrative poem written with a regular rhyme scheme.

    c)   This is a poem which tells a story and has a regular rhythm.

    d)   This is a poem which tells a story and has uniform stanza lengths. (2)

(Total for this section: 15 marks)

Section B

Answer the following questions in full sentences.

Re-read lines 8–15.

9   Explain how the appearance and movements of the snake are described through:

    a)   language choices (6)

    b)   sentence structure. (3)

Re-read lines 18–25.

10   How does the poet convey a sense of tension in these lines?

    Support your ideas with quotations. (6)

Re-read lines 26–31.

11   There are two voices in the poet's head. What is the tone of each voice?

    Explain your answer and support your ideas with short quotations. (4)

Re-read lines 32–36.

12   How do word choices show the poet's pleasure as he remembers the visit from the snake? (6)

(Total for this section: 25 marks)

Paper 1 (Reading): Poetry Practice Paper 3: From 'Snake'

Section C

13 How does the poet present his different feelings about the snake in this poem?

Develop three points of argument, each in a separate paragraph.

In your answer, you should explore:

- the telling of the story at the beginning of the poem
- the description of the snake's movements and appearance
- the concluding questions the poet asks himself.

Support each point with evidence; explain how the evidence demonstrates the poet's feelings about the snake. (10)

(Total marks for this section: 10)

(Total marks for paper: 50)

Paper 1 (Reading): Drama Practice Paper 1

From *Refugee Boy* by Benjamin Zephaniah, adapted for the stage by Lemn Sissay (2013)

> In the following play extract, Alem is a 14-year-old boy from Ethiopia/Eritrea sent to England to escape the violent civil war in his home country. He is taken from a children's home to live with a foster family, a family who will temporarily look after him.

The foster family.

The foster family: MR and MRS FITZGERALD and RUTH and ALEM.

Dining table.

MR FITZGERALD I put it down here. Then I went to the front room.

5   MRS FITZGERALD Have you looked in the front room?

MR FITZGERALD I've looked in the front room. Then I went in the front room. I took it into the front room.

RUTH Where did you last leave it?

MR FITZGERALD If I knew where I last left it ... Front room. Here.

10   MRS FITZGERALD Did you go to the toilet?

MR FITZGERALD I didn't go to the toilet.

MRS FITZGERALD Have a look in the front room again?

MR FITZGERALD It's not in the front room. It's got credit cards in it. Cash. And the picture. It's got the picture.

15   RUTH That picture of me. Dad!!!

ALEM Could you have left them with my bags?

RUTH When you start losing things it means you're going senile. Or there's other things on your mind. Other things to sort out.

MRS FITZGERALD Is that right, Ruth Fitzgerald?

20   *Alem quietly goes out.*

MR FITZGERALD I did bring it in, didn't I? If it's gone from the cab?! That's not funny, Ruth. One day you might have to look after us – must remember to dribble when I go senile.

RUTH Ugh!

MR FITZGERALD I've been robbed. Siobhan, I've been robbed. I knew it. I left it on the
25   dashboard, in the cab! Keys too. Where's my coat. Ruth, my coat.

Alem comes back in with his bag and Mr Fitzgerald's coat. Mr Fitzgerald's keys and wallet are in his coat.

ALEM Where shall I put these?

MR FITZGERALD Alem, you star. Alem knew where it was. Look at him. You'll be right at
30   home here, boy. Our luck has changed. He's good luck.

MRS FITZGERALD Is that right? Things get lost! A little attention to detail and we wouldn't lose them in the first place, would we now. Anyway, they're not lost, they're just elsewhere.

MR FITZGERALD Just elsewhere. Having a rest from the owner is what they're doing. A bit
35   like someone's homework.

MRS FITZGERALD Time for food.

Alem clasps his hands together and prays.

ALEM (*in Amharaic*) Dear God we give thanks for this food and for this family and please bring my father back to me as soon as possible so I can leave this place. Amen.

MR FITZGERALD Right. Right. Siobhan?

MRS FITZGERALD Yes. Well. Let's eat and then we must talk about court[1]. Was it a good week, Alem?

RUTH They love him. Everyone's like, pleased to see him now. Now it's like he owns the place. He settled in much better than Themba. And he's made friends and he's funny too, Mum and …

MR FITZGERALD That's great, Ruth.

RUTH But I'm sure he can speak for himself.

ALEM It's. It's great. I have mathematics, English, sports and a timetable that instructs which lessons are where and my form is 3C.

MR FITZGERALD Court. Nobody has told me about court.

An awkward pause.

RUTH So what did I do at school today? I wrote an essay on Dickens is what I did!

MRS FITZGERALD Who the dickens was Dickens?

MR FITZGERALD Good question. Ruth, who the dickens is Dickens?

RUTH I am not telling you if that's the way you're going to be.

MR FITZGERALD Okay.

Silence.

RUTH Dickens was a writer who wrote books.

---

[1] court = a place where a legal decision will be made over Alem's future

Foundation and Paper 1 (Reading): Practice Papers

Section A

Read the extract from *Refugee Boy* by Benjamin Zephaniah, adapted for the stage by Lemn Sissay. Then, select the correct answer for each multiple-choice question.

Re-read lines 4–14.

1 What dramatic form and device is used?
   a) mime – not all the characters are speaking
   b) comedy – using repetition as the device
   c) tragedy – with the use of asides
   d) comedy – using understatement as the device (2)

Re-read lines 4–27.

2 Mr Fitzgerald has:
   a) left Alem's bag in the cab
   b) left his keys in the toilet
   c) lost his coat
   d) forgotten his wallet was in his coat. (1)

Re-read lines 36–39.

3 The audience can understand from Alem's prayer that he is:
   a) thankful but unhappy
   b) ungrateful and sad
   c) grateful and happy
   d) amusing and funny. (2)

Re-read lines 41–49.

4 Have the Fitzgeralds looked after other homeless children?
   a) Alem is the first child the family have had living with them.
   b) At least one other child had lived with the Fitzgeralds before.
   c) Alem joins another homeless child whom the Fitzgeralds call Ruth.
   d) The Fitzgeralds do not look after children, only provide meals. (2)

5 How has Alem settled at school?
   a) Alem has missed school as he was in court.
   b) Alem has not made friends but is amusing.
   c) Alem has settled well and enjoys following his school timetable.
   d) Alem is overwhelmed by all the subjects and finding his way around. (2)

Paper 1 (Reading): Drama Practice Paper 1: *Refugee Boy*

Re-read lines 51–56.

6   What is Ruth's reaction to her parents when she told them what she had been doing at school?

   a)   amused that her parents do not know who Dickens is

   b)   proud that she knows such a lot about literature

   c)   annoyed that they seem uninterested

   d)   upset at the joke about Dickens (2)

Look at the passage as a whole.

7   How long has Alem been in the Fitzgerald's house?

   a)   two days

   b)   one night

   c)   he has just arrived

   d)   he is not in the Fitzgerald's house (2)

8   The content of this scene is:

   a)   the chance meeting of two teenagers who attend the same school

   b)   a family arguing about problems with their teenage children

   c)   a child evacuee, escaping civil war, living with a family who will care for him

   d)   a boy who has escaped from a children's home and moves in with friends. (2)

(Total marks for this section: 15)

Section B

Answer the following questions in full sentences.

9   There are episodes of tension.

   Briefly explain the reason for the tension and how the playwright breaks the tension:

   a)   in lines 36–42 (4)

   b)   in lines 50–52. (4)

10   What signs are the audience given that Alem will be happy with his new life, or not?

   Explain your answer with details from the text. (5)

11   Consider the interaction between Mr and Mrs Fitzgerald.

   What does the audience learn of the relationship between them?

   Support your ideas with discussion of evidence from the whole text. (6)

12   How does the playwright present family life:

   a)   by the way the Fitzgeralds speak to each other? (3)

   b)   through the stage setting? (3)

(Total marks for this section: 25)

Foundation and Paper 1 (Reading): Practice Papers

Section C

13 How does the playwright/writer use the characters of Alem and Ruth to highlight a contrast between the two teenagers to the audience?

Develop three points of argument, each in a separate paragraph.

In your answer consider the contrast:

- through their actions
- through the way they speak to Mr and Mrs Fitzgerald
- through their attitudes to life.

Support each point with evidence; explain how the evidence highlights the contrast between the teenagers. (10)

(Total marks for this section: 10)

(Total marks for paper: 50)

Paper 1 (Reading): Drama Practice Paper 2

From *An Inspector Calls* by JB Priestley (1945)

In the following play extract, it is 1912. Mr Birling, a wealthy business owner, is at home celebrating the engagement of his daughter Sheila to Gerald Croft. His son, Eric, is also present. A police inspector has arrived to inform them of a young girl's death and to make enquiries.

GERALD I've never known an Eva Smith.

ERIC Neither have I.

SHEILA Was that her name? Eva Smith?

GERALD Yes.

5   SHEILA Never heard it before.

GERALD So where are you now, Inspector?

INSPECTOR Where I was before, Mr Croft. I told you – that like a lot of these young women, she'd used more than one name. She was still Eva Smith when Mr Birling sacked her – for wanting twenty-five shillings[1] a week instead of twenty-two and six. But after
10   that she stopped being Eva Smith. Perhaps she'd had enough of it.

ERIC Can't blame her.

SHEILA (*to BIRLING*) I think it was a mean thing to do. Perhaps that spoilt everything for her.

BIRLING Rubbish! (*to INSPECTOR*) Do you know what happened to this girl after she left
15   my works?

INSPECTOR Yes. She was out of work for the next two months. Both her parents were dead, so that she'd no home to go back to. And she hadn't been able to save much out of what Birling and Company had paid her. So that after two months, with no work, no money coming in, and living in lodgings[2], with no relatives to help her, few friends, lonely, half-
20   starved, she was feeling desperate.

SHEILA (*warmly*) I should think so. It's a rotten shame.

INSPECTOR There are a lot of young women living that sort of existence in every city and big town in this country, Miss Birling. If there weren't, the factories and warehouses wouldn't know where to look for cheap labour[3]. Ask your father.

25   SHEILA But these girls aren't cheap labour – they're *people*.

INSPECTOR (*drily*) I've had that notion myself from time to time. In fact, I've thought it would do us all a bit of good if sometimes we tried to put ourselves in the place of these young women counting their pennies in their dingy little back bedrooms.

SHEILA Yes I expect it would. But what happened to her then?

30   INSPECTOR She had what seemed to her a wonderful stroke of luck. She was taken on in a shop – and a good shop too – Milwards.

SHEILA Milwards! We go there – in fact, I was there this afternoon (*archly to GERALD*) for your benefit.

GERALD (*smiling*) Good.

35   SHEILA Yes, she was lucky to get taken on at Milwards.

INSPECTOR That's what she thought. And it happened that at the beginning of December that year – nineteen-ten – there was a good deal of influenza[4] about, and Milwards suddenly

---

1 shillings = pre-decimal money – there were 20 shillings in a pound

2 lodgings = a rented room, perhaps in someone's house

3 cheap labour = workers

4 influenza = flu

found themselves short-handed. So that gave her her chance. It seems she liked working there. It was a nice change from a factory. She enjoyed being among pretty clothes, I've no
40   doubt. And now she felt she was making a good fresh start. You can imagine how she felt.

SHEILA Yes, of course.

INSPECTOR After about a couple of months, just when she felt she was settling down nicely, they told her she'd have to go.

BIRLING Not doing her work properly?

45   INSPECTOR There was nothing wrong with the way she was doing her work. They admitted that.

BIRLING There must have been something wrong.

INSPECTOR All she knew was – that a customer complained about her – and so she had to go.

SHEILA (*staring at him, agitated*) When was this?

50   INSPECTOR (*impressively*) At the end of January – last year.

SHEILA What – what did this girl look like?

INSPECTOR If you'll come over here, I'll show you.

He moves nearer a light – perhaps standard lamp- and she crosses to him. He produces the photograph. She looks at it closely, recognises it with a little cry, gives a half-stifled sob,
55   *and then runs out. The INSPECTOR puts the photograph back into his pocket and stares speculatively after her. The other three stare in amazement for a moment.*

BIRLING What's the matter with her?

ERIC She recognised her from the photograph, didn't she?

INSPECTOR Yes.

60   BIRLING Why the devil did you want to go upsetting the child like that?

INSPECTOR I didn't do it. She's upsetting herself.

BIRLING Well – why – why?

INSPECTOR I don't know – yet. That's something I have to find out.

BIRLING (*still angrily*) Well – if you don't mind – I'll find out first.

65   GERALD Shall I go to her?

BIRLING (*moving*) No, leave this to me. I must also have a word with my wife – tell her what's happening. (*Turns at door, staring at INSPECTOR angrily*) We were having a nice little family celebration tonight. And a nasty mess you've made of it now, haven't you?

Paper 1 (Reading): Drama Practice Paper 2: *An Inspector Calls*

Section A

Read the extract from *An Inspector Calls* by JB Priestley.

Then, select the correct answer for each multiple-choice question.

Re-read the introduction.

1 Which statement is correct?

    a) It is 1912 and Mr Birling is celebrating the engagement of his daughter to Eric.

    b) It is early in the twentieth century and Mr Birling is celebrating his birthday.

    c) It is in the nineteenth century and Mr Birling is celebrating his engagement.

    d) It is 1912 and Mr Birling is celebrating the engagement of his daughter to Gerald. (2)

Re-read lines 1–6.

2 The purpose of these lines is to inform the audience that:

    a) the victim was Eva Smith and none of them has heard her name

    b) the victim was Eva Smith and Sheila has heard her name

    c) the victim was Eva Smith and all of them have heard her name

    d) the victim was Eva Smith and the Inspector does not know her name. (2)

Re-read lines 7–24.

3 Why was Eva Smith sacked by Mr Birling?

    a) because she had changed her name

    b) because she asked for a little more money

    c) because she asked for twice as much money

    d) because she did not work well (1)

4 Why does the Inspector say: 'Ask your father'? (line 24)

    a) because he wants Sheila to admire and look up to her father

    b) because he knows that Mr Birling is a kind and generous employer

    c) because he knows that Mr Birling employs young women and pays them very little

    d) because he admires the way that Mr Birling employs young girls in his business (2)

Re-read lines 30–40.

5 What was the 'stroke of luck' for Eva Smith?

    a) She was employed by the restaurant Milwards as they needed more staff.

    b) She was employed by the shop Milwards as it was short-staffed due to sickness.

    c) She was employed by Mr Birling again and he paid her more.

    d) She was employed by the shop Milwards but became sick and had to leave. (2)

Foundation and Paper 1 (Reading): Practice Papers

6 Why does the Inspector think that she enjoyed working there?
   a) because it was a good shop and she liked the people she worked with
   b) because she liked working with clothes and serving people
   c) because it was a change from a factory job and was a fresh start
   d) because it was a change from a factory job and she liked serving food (2)

Re-read lines 42–48.

7 Eva left Milwards because:
   a) she was bored with selling clothes
   b) she did not work hard enough
   c) she became very sick with influenza
   d) a customer did not like her service. (2)

Re-read lines 53–56.

8 Which statement best describes why the playwright includes so much detail in the stage directions?
   a) It is an important moment in the scene and he wants to inform the producer how to stage it.
   b) It is an unimportant moment in the scene and so dialogue is not necessary here.
   c) It is an unimportant moment in the scene and he wants to give the audience a rest from listening.
   d) It is an important moment where the characters are moving into new positions. (2)

(Total marks for this section: 15)

Section B

Answer the following questions in full sentences.

From lines 1–15:

9 a) What is learnt about the personalities of Sheila and her father? (6)
   b) How can their relationship be described? (2)

Re-read lines 14–28.

10 How does the Inspector try to persuade his listeners to feel sympathy for Eva Smith?
   Find three examples and support your ideas with details from the text. (6)

Re-read lines 42–56.

11 How does the playwright create dramatic tension in these lines? (5)

Re-read from line 57 to the end.

12 Look closely at Mr Birling's speeches.
   Suggest reasons why he might speak to the Inspector in this way. (6)

(Total marks for this section: 25)

Paper 1 (Reading): Drama Practice Paper 2: *An Inspector Calls*

Section C

13 How does the playwright, JB Priestley, use the role of the Inspector to make this scene dramatic and thought-provoking for the audience?

Develop three points of argument, each in a separate paragraph.

In your answer, you should explore:

- his role as storyteller
- the other characters' reactions to Eva's story
- his comments about Eva Smith's life as a working girl.

Support each point with evidence; explain how the evidence adds dramatic and thought-provoking interest for the audience. (10)

(Total marks for this section: 10)

(Total marks for paper: 50)

Paper 1 (Reading): Drama Practice Paper 3

From *Forty Years On* by Alan Bennett (1968)

> In the following play extract, it is 1958 and the Headmaster is retiring after 40 years of service to the school. To celebrate, the staff and boys are putting on a play (which includes references to the First World War) in the school hall. It is the interval and the cast are having refreshments.
>
> Staff: The Headmaster, Matron (Molly) and Mr Franklin (who will be the new Headmaster)
>
> Boys: Leadbetter, Cartwright, Wigglesworth, Skinner, Tupper

1 modicum = a small amount

MATRON Headmaster, can I replenish you?

HEADMASTER Just a modicum[1], Matron, thank you.

MATRON You'll be shedding a few tears tonight, Headmaster, handing over the ship after so long.

5 HEADMASTER Retirement offers its own challenge, Matron. A chance to take up the slack of the mind, savour the rich broth of a lifetime's experience. Of course I'm not going far. I want to be within striking distance of the boys. ... Biting your nails, Leadbetter? Have you no moral sense at all?

MATRON I don't know what Mr Franklin will do without you.

2 corporal punishment = physical punishment

10 HEADMASTER Don't you? The first thing he will do is abolish corporal punishment[2], the second thing he'll do is abolish compulsory games. And the third thing he'll do is abolish the cadet corps[3]. Those are the three things liberal schoolmasters always do, Matron, the first opportunity they get. They think it makes the sensitive boys happy. In my experience sensitive boys are never happy anyway, so what is the point? Excuse me.

3 cadet corps = a group of schoolchildren receiving basic military training

15 *He has seen two boys who have donned gas masks and are larking about with them, running at each other like bulls. He suddenly comes between them and peers in through the talc[4].*

Skinner! Tupper!

Skinner and Tupper are not in fact the boys in the gas masks but are up to no good in the gallery where, hearing their names, they stand up guiltily.

4 talc = short for talcum powder used in drama when wearing props to prevent sweat

20 SKINNER/TUPPER Here, sir!

The Headmaster is nonplussed.

HEADMASTER No. No. I know those ears. Filthy! Wigglesworth, Cartwright. You can just stay like that the pair of you, until I tell you to take them off.

(*The focus of the action changes for a short while and then returns to the two boys and* 25 *Franklin.*)

Franklin comes across the two boys standing waiting in their gas masks.

FRANKLIN And what may I ask are you two comedians doing? If you don't get those gas masks off in three seconds flat, you'll be wearing them all night. Sorry Headmaster, did I balk[5] you of your prey?

5 balk = to deny, (in this context) to prevent or hinder

30 HEADMASTER Would it be impossibly naïve and old-fashioned of me to ask what it is you are trying to achieve in this impudent charade?

FRANKLIN You could say that we are trying to shed the burden of the past.

HEADMASTER Shed it? Why must we shed it? Why not shoulder it. Memories are not shackles, Franklin, they are garlands.

35 FRANKLIN We're too tied to the past. We want to be free to look to the future. The future comes before the past.

HEADMASTER Nonsense. The future comes after the past. Otherwise it couldn't be the future. Mind you, I liked that last bit, the bit that I read.* Was it true?

FRANKLIN Truth is a matter of opinion, really, isn't it, Headmaster?

HEADMASTER Did they actually go down there to that country house*?

FRANKLIN No.

HEADMASTER Oh, so it was a lie?

FRANKLIN It was a lie in the true sense of the word.

HEADMASTER You still like to sail a bit close to the knuckle, don't you? It won't be for much longer. It's very easy to be daring and outspoken, Franklin, but once you're at the helm the impetus will pass. Authority is a leaden cope[6]. You will be left behind, however daring and outspoken you are. You will be left behind, just as I have been left behind. Though when you fall as far behind as I have, you become a character. The mists of time lend one a certain romance. One thing at least I can say. While I have been Headmaster, Albion House has always been a going concern. Whether that will continue I am not sure. It depends on you, Franklin. But I am not sure of anything nowadays. I am lost. I am adrift. Everywhere one looks, decadence. I saw a bishop with a moustache the other day.

FRANKLIN It had to come. Molly, see if you can get the Old Man out of the way for the first bit or he'll be breezing onto the stage again.

MATRON Headmaster, I wonder if you'd come up to the San[7] to have a look at Dishforth? Not a pleasant sight at the best of times but he's a bit on the pasty side.

HEADMASTER Can I be spared?

FRANKLIN I think we'll just about manage.

---

* 'That last bit, the bit that I read.'; 'country house': these were mentioned earlier in the play

6 cope = a long, weighty cloak worn by clergymen

7 San = short for sanitarium meaning the sick room

Foundation and Paper 1 (Reading): Practice Papers

Section A

Read this extract from *Forty Years On* by Alan Bennett.

Then, select the correct answer for each multiple-choice question.

For question 7, provide a short answer in a full sentence.

Re-read lines 1–9.

1. Matron can here be described as:
   a) offhand, rude and uncaring
   b) polite, understanding and supportive
   c) polite and sympathetic, but unsupportive
   d) courteous, but unsympathetic and unsupportive. (1)

2. The phrase 'handing over the ship' (line 3) is:
   a) a simile to explain that the Headmaster is going on a retirement cruise
   b) a metaphor to explain that the Headmaster is giving away a model of a ship
   c) a metaphor to explain that the Headmaster is retiring and passing on the school to a new head
   d) a simile to explain that the Headmaster is retiring and passing on the school to a new head. (2)

3. What does the Headmaster mean when he says that he wants to be 'within striking distance' (line 7) of the boys when he retires?
   a) that the Headmaster wants to live next door to the boys' school when he retires
   b) that the Headmaster wants to live a long way away from the school
   c) that the Headmaster wants to live somewhere which is a good long walk to the school
   d) that the Headmaster is using the word 'striking' in two ways for comic effect (2)

Re-read lines 15–21.

4. Why is the Headmaster 'nonplussed'? (line 21)
   a) He is confused because he was not expecting those boys to reply to him.
   b) He is unable to see the boys who call out because they are outside.
   c) He gives up as he thinks the boys are playing a joke.
   d) He is put off by their reply and ignores them. (2)

Re-read lines 30–31.

5. The words 'this impudent charade' suggest that the Headmaster thinks the play is a:
   a) thoughtful mime
   b) ridiculous game
   c) disrespectful farce
   d) serious performance. (2)

Paper 1 (Reading): Drama Practice Paper 3: *Forty Years On*

Re-read lines 32–38.

6   Which statement best describes the Headmaster's and Franklin's point of view?

　　a)   They both think the past should be forgotten; it is the future that matters.

　　b)   Franklin thinks the past should be forgotten; the Headmaster thinks the past matters.

　　c)   Franklin thinks the past is important; the Headmaster thinks the future is more important.

　　d)   They both think that the past is important; the future is unimportant. (2)

Re-read line 46.

7   Write down what you think 'Authority is a leaden cope' means? (2)

Re-read lines 57–58.

8   What is the tone of the final line?

　　a)   doubtful

　　b)   sarcastic

　　c)   thoughtful

　　d)   sympathetic (2)

(Total marks for this section: 15)

Section B

Answer the following questions in full sentences.

Re-read lines 5–6.

9   How does the Headmaster use imagery to describe the 'challenge' of retirement? (5)

Re-read lines 10–14.

10   Explain what is revealed about the Headmaster as a teacher. (4)

Re-read lines 15–23.

11   What comic effects are achieved in these lines? Support your ideas with details from the text. (4)

Re-read lines 22–31.

12   a)   Why is there tension between the Headmaster and Franklin? (2)

　　b)   How is this tension made evident in the way they speak to each other? (4)

Re-read lines 44–52.

13   Suggest how the audience's feelings towards the Headmaster might evolve during this speech. (6)

(Total marks for this section: 25)

Foundation and Paper 1 (Reading): Practice Papers

Section C

14 How does the playwright, Alan Bennett, enable the audience to develop a different view of the Headmaster, as a teacher, than he does of himself?

Develop three points of argument, each in a separate paragraph.

You might like to consider:

- how the Headmaster views himself
- how he is viewed by the audience in the gas mask episode with the boys and Franklin
- how he is viewed by the audience in his interactions with Franklin and Matron at the end of the extract.

Support each point with evidence; explain how the evidence enables the audience to gain a different view of the Headmaster. (10)

(Total marks for this section: 10)

(Total marks for paper: 50)

Paper 2 Writing: Practice Papers

Introduction
ISEB 13+ writing question papers start with the following information:

> Time allowed: 1 hour 15 minutes
>
> Answer two questions from the choice of four.
>
> You should spend 30 minutes on each question.
>
> In addition, you have 15 minutes for:
> - reading the paper
> - planning your responses
> - checking your work carefully.

The writing titles, common to both Foundation and Paper 1 candidates, are designed to test a range of writing styles, both fiction and non-fiction. Choose any two options from a choice of four.

The 'styles' you may be asked to write in include: narrative, descriptive, informative, discursive or persuasive and will take different 'forms'.

A guide to styles and forms

Narrative: this is a story or part of a story based on believable events, characters and settings.

It could be reflective or imaginative and not necessarily based on your own experience; or it could be a combination of realism and imagination.

Descriptive: the writing will describe a person, place or an event/journey (real or imagined) so that the reader can clearly visualise, and enter into, your/the writer's experience.

Informative: this form could include: a news report, article or letter; an evaluative report or a study drawing conclusions; an information pamphlet, blog post or speech informing the audience of an issue and making recommendations.

It may be necessary to explain/advise/inform, pulling together relevant information such as opinions, facts, viewpoints and statements.

Discursive: the purpose is to present objectively two balanced sides to a topic. Your opinion may be required in the conclusion.

The form could include: a written balanced argument, a letter, an article, a speech, a report or a study drawing conclusions.

Persuasive: the purpose is to persuade the audience to adopt the writer's point of view or to debate a topic.

The form could include: a speech, an article, a letter (or a letter of complaint), a pamphlet or a blog post.

See ISEB document 'Paper 2 (Writing) in the Appendix and annotated writing sample responses (pages 141–152) which cover all the above styles.

Writing strategies and tips
Timing
In the exam, you will have 37.5 minutes for each of the two writing tasks, which will include planning and checking time. Try to spend the advised time (30 minutes) on writing the task so that you show

Paper 2 Writing: Practice Papers

yourself off to the full. As you have not got long, simple and well-expressed ideas will be more effective than complicated but unfinished responses. You might like to start with the one which you think will be your strongest.

Reading the paper and choosing writing tasks

Read all the choices carefully and thoughtfully. Play to your strengths to give yourself the opportunity to shine with your own writing voice in each essay.

Things to think about:

Story: the obvious might work well. But consider exploring an interesting approach to the title. For example, 'Climbing the Mountain' could be used literally or the character could be faced with a challenge.

The writing will be prompted by a title, quotation, proverb or sentence.

Descriptive writing: make sure that you have enough material in your head to sustain the writing. For example, in description you could change from day to night or sunshine to rain.

Also, keeping the focus wide might help. For example if 'Fire' is a title, you could write about the Great Fire of London rather than the fire in your sitting room.

Non-fiction writing: make sure you have enough information and ideas about the topic.

If there are bullets or prompts in non-fiction titles, use these as they are there to help you with your ideas and the structure of your writing.

Do not be put off if the title looks long or is a lot to read – it may be the most straightforward, giving the most help.

Addressing the question

Read the question at least twice, then underline or highlight the key words in the question to ensure that your writing is relevant, responds precisely and delivers on the chosen task and purpose. Also, make sure you identify, and then write to, the correct audience.

Planning your responses

This is a vital stage. Having chosen a title/task and understood what you have to do, you will need to plan. Choosing and planning may take up to five minutes. Do not be tempted to skip the planning stage in your anxiety to start writing – whatever anybody else in the room is doing!

You may have a preferred way of planning. For example:

- an ideas map
- bullet points
- a story mountain
- a sketch
- numbered paragraphs.

Go with what you feel most comfortable but be sure to sequence and embellish your ideas so that you have a clear progression showing direction and purpose. It is not sufficient to jot down random thoughts. In an exam situation, you need to know where your writing is going. Do not assume the reader is in your head and automatically follows your direction.

Use this planning time to secure your ideas on paper so that, when you come to the writing stage, your mind is freed up to concentrate on how you write rather than what you write.

A plan will also be helpful as a way of monitoring your progress against the time available. With practice, you will understand how much you will be able to write in the time. As well as ensuring you have enough to write about, also be sure you are not attempting too much and that your ideas are manageable for 30 minutes' writing. In particular, keep a story plot relatively simple. It may be better to choose a small event, which is well described. You need to be able to show off your writing skills in this time.

Introduction

There will be little time for reviewing and editing, so this planning time will enable you to sift your ideas carefully, making sure they work. If you do not have enough ideas to sustain your writing, better to abandon this title now and move on quickly to another, rather than realising halfway through when it is too late. If you have too many ideas to explore in the given time, a cull might be needed at this planning stage. Use your best and strongest ideas first, in case you run short of time.

Practise whether you prefer to plan both titles/choices before you start to write, or plan one and write that response before tackling the other. See which works best for you.

In the answer section of the book there are some model writing answers. Each one has its own plan which will give you some specific and practical help.

Checking your work carefully

This is an important stage, and you are expected to leave time for this. Re-read your work, looking out for:

- spelling mistakes, including names of characters and places
- missing words
- a variety of accurate and sufficient punctuation
- consistency of tense and narrative voice
- paragraphing
- your own frequent errors.

Be sure your work is clear and easy to understand for your marker, who may have many scripts to consider.

See the Writing Paper answer section for writing mark schemes, further guidance and annotated sample responses.

On the ISEB 13+ writing question papers the following advice is given:

> Credit will be given for accurate spelling, punctuation and grammar, choices of effective vocabulary and clear presentation of your ideas.

Spelling: try to spell with accuracy but not at the expense of using interesting vocabulary. The correct spelling of high frequency words and homophones is important.

Punctuation: try to show off an accurate range of punctuation. This will enhance the communication of your ideas.

Use commas, semicolons, colons, dashes, brackets and apostrophes with confidence. Remember that dialogue should be punctuated and laid out accurately.

This can be tricky and will need practice.

Grammar: communicate your ideas clearly using varied and accurate sentence structures.

Choices of effective vocabulary: make your vocabulary choices appropriate to the task, sophisticated and engaging. Good vocabulary is impressive.

Clear presentation of your ideas: presentation is important as it is your marker's first impression of your work.

Your handwriting should be consistently well-formed in a clear style, with regular sizing and spacing. Take care with the demarcation of paragraphs. Crossing out should be limited and neat.

However, 'clear presentation of your ideas' requires more than handwriting. Time well used at the beginning to plan and structure your ideas will provide clarity to the final piece.

Checking technical accuracy and sense at the end will be time well-used to ensure you are a clear communicator.

See the Writing Paper answer section and the sample answers for further guidance.

Paper 2 Writing: Practice Papers

Writing Practice Paper 1

Write on any TWO of the following titles or prompts.

Each one is worth 25 marks.

Credit will be given for accurate spelling, punctuation and grammar, choices of effective vocabulary and clear presentation of your ideas.

1. Write a story with **one** of the following titles:
   EITHER
   'The End of the Road'
   OR
   'The Open Door'
   OR
   'The Hidden Pathway'
2. Write a persuasive letter to your headteacher to convince them that a new outdoor activity should be taught as part of the curriculum or as a club.
3. Write a description of the 30 minutes before an exam.
4. Write an information pamphlet for the visitors to a family holiday attraction which you know well.

(Total marks for paper: 50)

Writing Practice Paper 2

Write on any TWO of the following titles or prompts.

Each one is worth 25 marks.

Credit will be given for accurate spelling, punctuation and grammar, choices of effective vocabulary and clear presentation of your ideas.

1. Think of a place you know well and describe it after dark.
2. Write a blog post about the joys of owning and caring for a pet.
3. Write a story which includes **one** of the following sentences:
   EITHER
   'And then there was one.'
   OR
   'My pockets were empty.'
   OR
   'It was the wrong address.'
4. Write an article for your school magazine in which you discuss the relevance of libraries in today's world of technology.

(Total marks for paper: 50)

Writing Practice Paper 3

Write on any TWO of the following titles or prompts.

Each one is worth 25 marks.

Credit will be given for accurate spelling, punctuation and grammar, choices of effective vocabulary and clear presentation of your ideas.

1. Write a description of an imaginary creature, place or person.
2. 'Children, not adults, should decide how much screen time to enjoy.'
   Write an article for your school magazine in which you discuss this statement and give your views.
   (See sample answer.)
3. Write about a time when you had to swallow your pride.
4. Write an information pamphlet on how to:
   EITHER
   create a bug hotel
   OR
   build a den.

(Total marks for paper: 50)

Writing Practice Paper 4

Write on any TWO of the following titles or prompts.

Each one is worth 25 marks.

Credit will be given for accurate spelling, punctuation and grammar, choices of effective vocabulary and clear presentation of your ideas.

1. Write a report drawing conclusions about an environmental or ecological issue in your local area.
   (See sample answer.)
2. Write a letter to leave with a time capsule buried in your garden.
3. Write a description of your journey to school:
   EITHER
   in the snow
   OR
   in a rainstorm.
4. 'Losing My Way'
   Write a story using this title.

(Total marks for paper: 50)

Paper 2 Writing: Practice Papers

Writing Practice Paper 5

Write on any TWO of the following titles or prompts.

Each one is worth 25 marks.

Credit will be given for accurate spelling, punctuation and grammar, choices of effective vocabulary and clear presentation of your ideas.

1. 'We were lucky indeed that day.'
   Use this sentence as the last line of a story.
   (See sample answer.)
2. 'Being one of life's team players ... is it always a good thing?'
   Explore your views on this topic.
3. Write a description of someone who lives or works in your local area.
4. 'Three Brilliant Birthday Party Ideas For Free'
   Write a blog with your top suggestions.

(Total marks for paper: 50)

Writing Practice Paper 6

Write on any TWO of the following titles or prompts.

Each one is worth 25 marks.

Credit will be given for accurate spelling, punctuation and grammar, choices of effective vocabulary and clear presentation of your ideas.

1. Describe a busy street first thing in the morning and in the quiet of the evening.
2. Your school wants to appoint a 'Kindness Monitor' whose job it will be to try to help the school towards a culture of kindness.
   Write a letter to your headteacher, recommending why you think you should be appointed and what things you might do.
   (See sample answer.)
3. Write a news report about a water rescue.
4. Write in any way you like on **one** of the following titles:
   - 'Locked In'
   - 'Locked Out'
   - 'Locked Up'

(Total marks for paper: 50)

Writing Practice Paper 7

Write on any TWO of the following titles or prompts.

Each one is worth 25 marks.

Credit will be given for accurate spelling, punctuation and grammar, choices of effective vocabulary and clear presentation of your ideas.

1. Write a description of a scene where the weather plays an important role.
   (See sample answer.)
2. Write a story which begins or ends with:
   EITHER
   a text message
   OR
   a scream
   OR
   an apology.
3. Write a blog about an outdoor activity which you enjoy.
   (See sample answer.)
4. Concerning global issues such as the environment, health and famine often dominate the media.
   In contrast, write a discussion piece about something which gives you hope for the future.

(Total marks for paper: 50)

Writing Practice Paper 8

Write on any TWO of the following titles or prompts.

Each one is worth 25 marks.

Credit will be given for accurate spelling, punctuation and grammar, choices of effective vocabulary and clear presentation of your ideas.

1. 'This house believes that teaching handwriting is a thing of the past.'
   Write a speech for a school debate, in which you argue either for or against this statement.
2. Write in any way you wish on **one** of the following proverbs:
   - 'Actions speak louder than words.'
   - 'When the going gets tough, the tough get going.'
   - 'Practice makes perfect.'
3. Describe a journey you have made which brings back pleasant or unpleasant memories.
4. Write a report, drawing conclusions, about how to stay safe with your friends:
   EITHER
   in an urban environment
   OR
   in a rural environment.

(Total marks for paper: 50)

Paper 2 Writing: Practice Papers

Writing Practice Paper 9

Write on any TWO of the following titles or prompts.

Each one is worth 25 marks.

Credit will be given for accurate spelling, punctuation and grammar, choices of effective vocabulary and clear presentation of your ideas.

1. 'Every day I had to go there. Every day I hoped it would be different.'
   Continue this story.
2. Write a description of yourself through the eyes of:
   EITHER
   a teacher
   OR
   a friend
   OR
   a family member.
3. 'Boredom is beneficial'
   Write a speech, for or against this statement, to deliver to your school assembly. Try to be as persuasive as you can.
   (See sample answer.)
4. Write a letter of complaint to:
   EITHER
   a cinema
   OR
   a sports facility in which you outline the reasons for your disappointing experience.

(Total marks for paper: 50)

Writing Practice Paper 10

Write on any TWO of the following titles or prompts.

Each one is worth 25 marks.

Credit will be given for accurate spelling, punctuation and grammar, choices of effective vocabulary and clear presentation of your ideas.

1. Write a story using **one** of the following titles:
   - 'Watching and Waiting'
   - 'Missing'
   - 'The Parting'
2. 'How to cope with a public performance.'
   Write a blog on this subject.
3. Write an article for your school magazine about a person from history that you particularly admire.
4. 'It was the best of school days; it was the worst of school days.'
   Describe one such day in your school life.

(Total marks for paper: 50)

Writing Practice Paper 11

Write on any TWO of the following titles or prompts.

Each one is worth 25 marks.

Credit will be given for accurate spelling, punctuation and grammar, choices of effective vocabulary and clear presentation of your ideas.

1. Your local councillor has written to your school asking for volunteers to support the elderly with computer technology.
   Write a letter, starting 'Dear Councillor', suggesting why you think you would be suitable for the role.
2. Write a report for your headteacher about a recent school trip you have been on.
   In your report consider both its benefits and drawbacks.
3. 'My Pride and Joy'
   Write in any way you wish using this title.
4. 'She walked away in the opposite direction.'
   Use this sentence either to begin or to end a story.

(Total marks for paper: 50)

Writing Practice Paper 12

Write on any TWO of the following titles or prompts.

Each one is worth 25 marks.

Credit will be given for accurate spelling, punctuation and grammar, choices of effective vocabulary and clear presentation of your ideas.

1. Imagine you are part of life on Mars. Describe it.
2. 'We can do this together. We can play our part. We can help each other out.'
   Write a speech using these ideas to present :
   EITHER
   to a sports team
   OR
   to the cast of a play or a music group.
3. What do you think has been the greatest ever discovery?
   Write an article for your school magazine in which you explain your choice.
4. Write a story using **one** of the following titles:
   - 'Footprints'
   - 'Darkening Skies'
   - 'The Suitcase'

(Total marks for paper: 50)

Exam Practice Answers

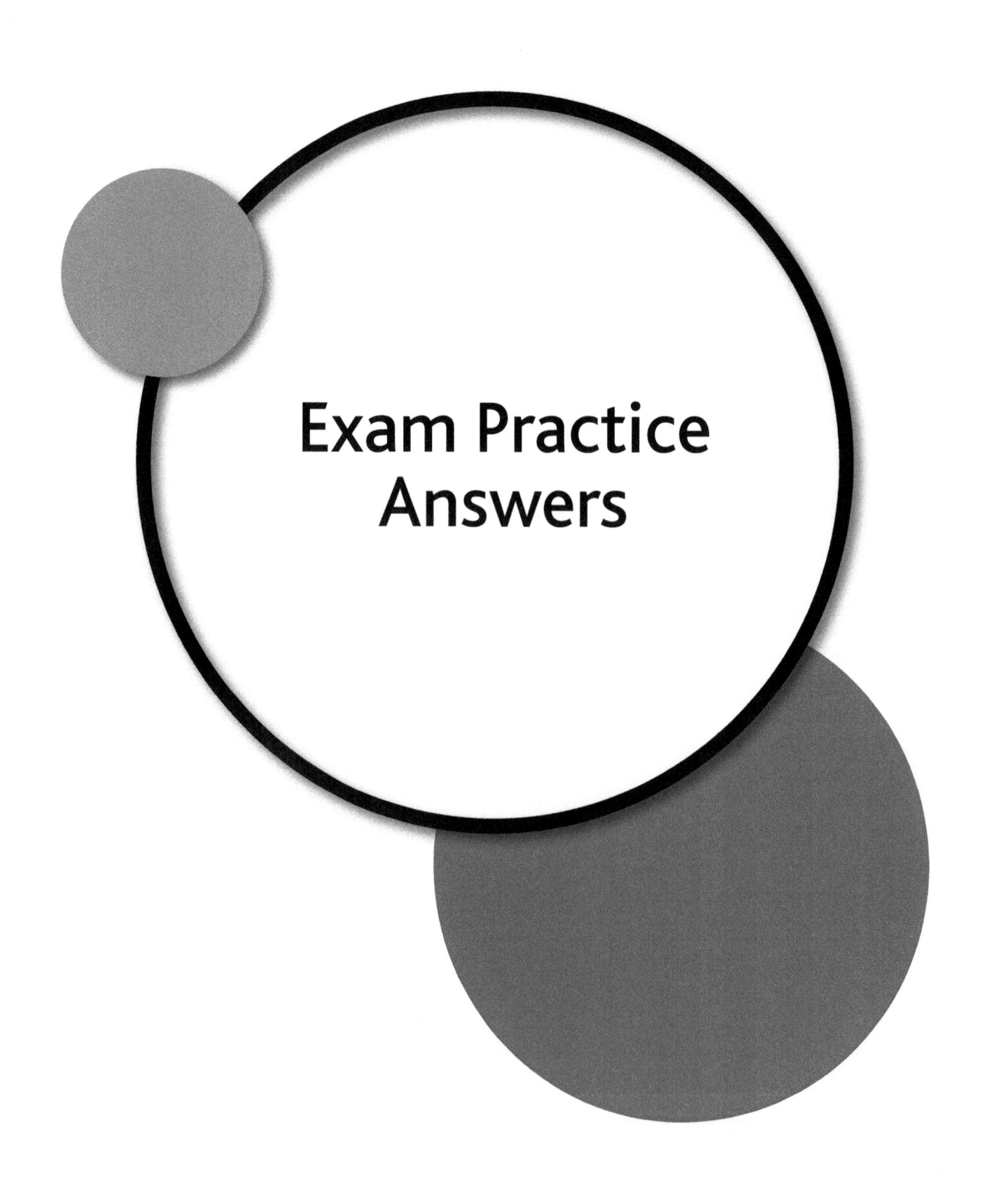

Foundation and Paper 1 (Reading): Practice Paper Answers

Guidance for students, teachers and parents

This section aims to help you mark responses to the practice papers with confidence.

The detailed analysis that follows should be a time saver when marking. It provides the key requirements of answers, together with evidence and explanations, all carefully identified. The answers form 'a suggested, not a prescriptive mark scheme' as explained on the front of the ISEB answer specimen papers. It is not possible to write a hard and fast mark scheme for English, unlike some other subjects. We acknowledge that candidates may discover the unusual and that teachers prefer the autonomy to mark in their own way.

In Section B, you will notice that some answers are awarded marks according to the level of understanding and depth of response. There is a staged approach to this: 'straightforward', 'developed', 'integrated', 'insightful'. To gain maximum marks in these questions try to show off understanding and depth of thought.

Foundation: All guidance for Section C answer is on the answer grid; the grid below is only relevant for Paper 1.

Paper 1: There are two answer grids that you will need to follow when marking Section C. Each text has its own Section A, B and C answer grids. In addition, Section C has a generic answer grid (see below).

Read through the ISEB mark bands in the chart below (from 1–3, 4–6, 7–8 and 9–10) to show you how to improve your Section C (Question 13/14) Extended Writing response.

Marks	
9–10	• the argument is incisive, insightful, articulate and logically structured
	• evidence is illuminating and selected to enable deeper analysis
	• points are supported and developed with close analysis of the effects of language and form
7–8	• clear and insightful points of argument, logically structured
	• evidence is carefully selected to support each point
	• some discussion of the writer's language choices to develop argument
4–6	• three clear points of argument, although there may be some overlap/repetition
	• an attempt to provide evidence for each point
	• some straightforward discussion of the evidence
1–3	• an attempt to respond
	• there is evidence of some relevant thought

Foundation and Paper 1 (Reading): Practice Paper Answers

Foundation: Practice Paper 1: *The Endless Steppe*

Section A

1 c) The word 'as' indicates a simile. Esther wakes up feeling her surroundings are unusually dark. (1)

2 d) Esther has minimal tools for school: 'my little notebook and small stub of a pencil' (line 4) and her clothes are not warm or sturdy enough for the Siberian weather: 'thin, little blouse', 'shoes ... pinching ... beginning to crack'. (lines 7–8) (2)

3 a) She is not worried by walking alone to school, but anxious about learning in the Russian language on her first day: 'never occurred to me that for a child to walk alone ... too busy trying to rehearse the Russian alphabet'. (lines 11–13) (2)

4 b) Her welcome at the school was cold: 'looked at me so severely that my heart sank' (lines 15–16) and direct: 'It was as if she was reading ... determine some sort of punishment.' (lines 17–18) (2)

5 For 2 marks candidates must explain both 'soldier' and 'without a gun'. Esther feels ill-equipped as a student/very unprepared – lacking the tools she will need for the school tasks ahead of her. (2)

6 d) Esther finds the words difficult to understand: 'the Russian author's meaning that evaded me ... sea of strange letters' (lines 25–26); the girl next to her is reluctant to share the book: 'My class mate somehow managed to keep slipping it out of my field of vision' (lines 27–28); she feels her difficulties are revealed to the class when the teacher asks her a question so soon: 'To my horror, one question was directed at me.' (line 30) (2)

7 c) 'to be the queen bee' is a metaphor; 'and' is a connective. (2)

8 b) is false. Neither Raisa Nikitovna, the teacher, nor Svetlana, Esther's class mate, greet her with a friendly warmth. (2)

(Total of 15 marks available)

Section B

Q.	Answer	Mark	Additional guidance
9	*Any three of the following:* Esther has moved from Poland to Russia. Lives near the country: 'howl of a wolf way out in the country gave me my bearings'. (lines 2–3) Has few possessions/not much money: 'little notebook and a small stub of pencil, my only academic possessions'. (line 4) Has little money and so inadequate/poor clothes: 'thin, little blouse', 'my black leather shoes which were not only pinching but which were beginning to crack', 'one and only coat'. (lines 7–9) Lives with mother/mother has to work: 'Mother had to be at the bakery early that day'. (line 10)	3	1 mark for each point. Candidates may stay close to the language of the text.

Foundation: Practice Paper 1: *The Endless Steppe*

Q.	Answer	Mark	Additional guidance
10	Thin/inadequate clothes in very cold weather. (lines 7–9) Walking to school alone (lines 11–12): obviously an unusual sight as the road is deserted. 'down a deserted Siberian road' (lines 11–12): no other children walking to school. Clutching a notebook and pencil (line 10): no school bag. 'a few children in caps and coats were seated at their desks' (line 14): the weather was so cold, even inside children wore coats and hats.	4	Two details from text required. 2 marks available for each detail explained.
11 a)	*Answers may include:* *Esther:* - Nikitovna is judgemental: 'From Poland. Your Russian will be poor.' (line 17) - She has hard work ahead: 'It will be my task to see that you improve it.' (lines 18–19) - She wants Esther to realise it will be hard/teaches her a lesson by not giving her a book/asking her a question about the text, in front of the class. - Possibly disapproving: 'little notebook and a small stub of pencil', 'thin, little blouse', 'my black leather shoes which were not only pinching but which were beginning to crack', 'one and only coat'. (lines 4–9)	3	1 mark for noting simple recognition of how Raisa Nikitovna might feel towards Esther. 1 mark for any additional point linked to the text. Up to 3 marks, in total, for developed point(s) linked closely to the text.
b)	*Svetlana:* - Nikitovna may be approving of Svetlana: 'a very pretty girl with short blond hair, and eyes the special blue of northern countries'. (line 23) - She knows that she is responsible: 'She will share her books with Svetlana. Stand up Svetlana.' (line 34) - She favours Svetlana who is used to being the popular one: 'Svetlana wanted to be the queen bee'. (line 37)	3	1 mark for noting simple recognition of how Raisa Nikitovna might feel towards Svetlana. 1 mark for any additional point linked to the text. Up to 3 marks, in total, for developed point(s) linked closely to the text.
12	*Svetlana:* - She is the popular girl, who could make Esther's life difficult with other pupils/the teacher. - She will need to prove herself to Svetlana to win her over. *Raisa Nikitovna:* - She is a strict/unforgiving teacher, who already has not warmed to her. - She will need to work hard, and build on the little knowledge she already has, to show despite not having 'academic possessions', she can be a good student. *the Russian alphabet*: - It is a difficult alphabet, alien to Esther, that will be the key to learning. - Understanding this alphabet and learning to read and write fluently will help overcome the other two 'giants'.	6	1 mark for understanding why each seems a 'giant' to Esther. 1 mark for brief explanation how each might be slain.

Foundation and Paper 1 (Reading): Practice Paper Answers

Q.		Answer	Mark	Additional guidance
13		*Suggestions may include:*		
	a)	Brave: gets herself up, dressed and walks to school alone, despite along a cold, deserted road.	3	1 mark for straightforward impression.
		Determined: gets herself to school alone, additionally practises the Russian alphabet as she goes, in preparation for the day ahead.		1 mark for any additional point/development linked to the text.
		Mature: is understanding/uncomplaining that she must do this alone and try to make the most of the education on offer.		Up to 3 marks, in total, for developed point(s) linked closely to the text.
	b)	Brave/determined: despite a harsh reception in class. Although she cannot understand Russian, attempts to read and answer a question.	3	1 mark for straightforward impression.
		Mature/strong: identifies the problems ahead that she will need to deal with – her teacher, Svetlana and the Russian alphabet.		1 mark for any additional point/development linked to the text.
		Persistent: continues her efforts but tired once she reaches home and reflects on the first day.		Up to 3 marks, in total, for developed point(s) linked closely to the text.
		(Other alternatives for a) and b) may be offered but these are the principal options.)		
Total			25	

Section C

Q.	Answer	Mark	Additional guidance
14	**Ideas for Svetlana's diary may include:** • *Svetlana's observations about Esther:* She may note, and be critical of, her modest school equipment: 'little notebook and a small stub of a pencil'. (line 4) She may note her poor clothing, not suitable for the cold weather: 'thin, little blouse', 'shoes … pinching … beginning to crack', 'my one and only coat'. (lines 7–9) She may notice that Esther is not blond, 'with eyes the special blue of northern countries'. (line 23) (Reward inferences of Svetlana's disapproval from the outset of Esther's appearance.) • *Svetlana's feelings about her:* She is not Russian, as Svetlana is. Esther is not (initially) judged to be a clever girl: 'You must be Esther Rudomin. From Poland. Your Russian will be poor.' (line 17) She does not wish Esther to sit with her/to share her books with Esther: 'My class mate somehow managed to keep slipping it out of my field of vision'. (lines 27–28) She does not want Esther getting attention: 'The more attention I got in class, the more she sulked.' (line 36)	10	1 mark for writing from Svetlana's point of view, in the first person. Up to 3 marks for developing a response to each of the bullet points: 1 mark for including a straightforward reference to the ideas suggested by the bullet point and inferred from the text, in a diary style, including some thoughts/feelings. 2 marks for a more developed response to the ideas suggested by the bullet point, and clearly inferred from the text, in a diary style, including more detailed thoughts/feelings. 3 marks for a detailed and developed response; imaginative with good insight into Svetlana's

78

Foundation: Practice Paper 1: *The Endless Steppe*

Q.	Answer	Mark	Additional guidance
	Candidates may develop ideas that Svetlana sees Esther as an unwelcome intruder/threat, who may not be the sort of friend Svetlana might want; she may have been secretly pleased her teacher chose her to share books with Esther and be asked to stand up; she does not want Esther to take the attention away from her. • *Svetlana's thoughts about working with Esther in the future:* She did not want to help Esther out of class in any way and talks down to her: 'when I asked if I might come to her house and study with her. The answer was a sharp "No!" I would be allowed to go there to fetch books but when she had finished with them, but otherwise I could jolly well trot home and study alone.' (lines 38–40) (Reward a response that shows Svetlana very clearly does not want to make a friend of Esther; indeed she may choose to make her life difficult.)		thoughts/feelings, yet clearly drawn from the text, in a diary style. Candidates should write in Svetlana's voice – they should pick up that this will be sulky, selfish and superior. (Quotations given here are to support the marker, as candidates must pick up clues, but these are not required in the answer.)
Total		**10**	

Foundation and Paper 1 (Reading): Practice Paper Answers

Foundation: Practice Paper 2: *The Girl with a Pearl Earring*

Section A

1 b) Clearly stated in the introduction. (1)

2 c) This is a metaphor as there is no 'like' or 'as' (line 1). Griet's mother is looking at her. The man and woman are behind her. (2)

3 To score 2 marks candidates must explain the inference that Griet feels that her family are less important than the taller and richer visitors, as they are smaller. (2)

4 d) No other suggestions are applicable. (2)

5 c) The short sentence creates tension but having it in a paragraph of its own makes it stand out as well; the question asks for the best answer. (2)

6 b) The correct choice has two parts to it with these details explained: 'I could not say why I had laid the vegetables as I did' (line 39); 'I was too frightened to say so to a gentleman' (line 40) which would make her nervous of him. (2)

7 a) He shows interest in her up to, and beyond, this point; the other answers have no relevance. (2)

8 a) This is the only answer where the extract gives proof of both qualities: she notices small details about the visitors (observant) and she is polite (respectful) when the man questions her. (2)

(Total of 15 marks available)

Section B

Q.	Answer	Mark	Additional guidance
9	• 'Her collar needed straightening and was not as crisp as it could be.' (lines 6–7) Griet seems to like things to be neat and tidy: so the woman's collar offended her in two ways as she felt it 'needed straightening' and was 'not as crisp as it could be'. • 'The woman's face was … flashing at times, dull at others'. (line 10) This suggests that Griet found the woman hard to read as her eyes were sending mixed signals: bright and full of life but also lifeless and gloomy. • 'She made a show of watching me hard but could not fix her attention on me, her eyes darting about the room.' (lines 11–13) Griet feels she is insincere in her behaviour ('made a show …'); that the woman is not really interested in her as she did not look at her for long and her eyes moved swiftly around the room. • 'Well. She's not very big. Is she strong enough?' (line 17) As Griet seems to take care in her tasks and works hard, she might feel insulted by this suggestion that she is too small and weak for the maid's job. We already know that she feels sensitive about her height.	8	2 marks available for each explanation. Award 1 mark for a relevant but straightforward response. Award 2 marks for a more insightful, incisive and imaginative response to language. The quotation does not need to be written out.

Foundation: Practice Paper 2: *The Girl with a Pearl Earring*

Q.	Answer	Mark	Additional guidance
10	*Answers may include:*		
a)	She makes a short statement rather than asking a question; she calls Griet, 'the girl' rather than giving her a name; she speaks 'abruptly' meaning sharply or rudely; her words are monosyllabic as if she is not really interested.	2	Up to 2 marks for recognition of what she says and how she says it.
b)	It is as if Griet's mother is correcting her; she uses the same sentence structure but substitutes words for a more polite and warm effect as she does not like the woman's rude tone; she calls Griet her 'daughter' instead of 'girl' and she tells the woman Griet's name.	2	Up to 2 marks for explanation of any two or more points.
11	*What he looks like:* • 'The man was watching me, his eyes grey like the sea.' (line 26) • 'his expression was steady, in contrast to his wife's' (lines 26–27) • 'He had no beard or moustache, and I was glad, for it gave him a clean appearance.' (lines 27–28) • 'He wore … a fine lace collar.' (lines 28–29) *What the man says:* • '"Catharina," the man said calmly.' (line 21) • '"What have you been doing here, Griet?" he asked.' (line 31)	4	1 mark for each quotation. Explanations for the choices are not expected. Both what he looks like and what he says to be included.
12	*Answers may include:*		
a)	The man wants to find out more about her especially if she is going to be their maid because: • he is an artist so he is curious about/interested in the precise circle she makes with the vegetables when she lays them out • he is an artist so he is curious about/interested in how she arranges the colours of the vegetables • he wants to know why she has laid them out like that • he wants to know how her mind works • he is checking that she won't waste time and will work hard.	3	Three reasons why the man questions Griet expected for 3 marks.
b)	She means that certain colours (the orange carrots and the purple cabbage) clash when they are next to each other; to her eyes the colours do not look attractive together; shows a natural understanding of colours.	2	Award 1 mark for explaining personification in 'fight'. Award 1 mark for explaining which vegetables 'fight'.
13 a)	The lie is that instead of saying 'yes' she replies 'no' when he asks her if she spends much time setting out the vegetables before she makes soup with them.	1	Award 1 mark for understanding.
b)	She lies because she does not want the man to think she is lazy/wasting time instead of cooking.	1	Award 1 mark for understanding of 'idle' within answer.
c)	She looks down because her sister hears her lie, indicated by shaking her head. She feels ashamed of herself and sorry that her sister overhears.	2	Award 1 mark each for up to two reasons.
Total		**25**	

Foundation and Paper 1 (Reading): Practice Paper Answers

Section C

Q.	Answer	Mark	Additional guidance
14	*Ideas for the mothers' re-telling may include:* • *Her observations and reactions to the woman:* 　• The mother may notice the woman's height, her untidy appearance, the growing baby, 'her eyes darting about the room'. (lines 12–13) 　• She may dislike the woman's lack of interest in her, her abrupt manner of speaking, her criticism of Griet's size 'She's not very big', (line 17) her doubt that she will be up to the job 'Is she strong enough?', (line 17) and her dramatic reaction to the fallen knife 'The woman cried out.' (line 20) (Reward details about the woman's appearance and behaviour and the mother's reactions to them.) • *Her feelings towards Griet:* 　• She may feel anxious about how Griet behaves 'her eyes two warnings' (line 1) as the family needs Griet to get this job. 　• She may feel proud of Griet for being so polite 'nodded respectfully to the man and woman' (lines 15–16); sad that she will have to leave the home; worried that she will be with this woman whom neither she nor Griet seem to like; proud at the way Griet handles all the man's questions. (Reward empathetic observations about the situation her daughter is in and, perhaps, her sadness that she has to become a maid/move away.) • *Her thoughts about the man's questions/Griet's replies:* 　• She may think that he overdid the questions; that she did not like to see Griet feeling uncomfortable '"Oh no, sir," I replied confused.' (line 48); but pleased that he was showing an interest in her, unlike his wife. 　• She may feel proud at the way Griet handled the situation and questions when she could see her fear and discomfort; perhaps pleased (or embarrassed) that he noticed Griet's artistic qualities in her laying out of the vegetables 'Are they laid out in the order in which they will go into the soup?' (lines 37–38) (Reward writing which shows that the mother was able to understand what Griet was going through during this encounter with the man.) (Reward development and explanation of ideas that can be inferred clearly from the text.)	10	1 mark for telling the story using the first-person perspective, from the mother's point of view. Up to 3 marks for developing a response to each of the bullet points: 1 mark for including a straightforward reference to the ideas suggested by the bullet point and inferred from the text. 2 marks for a more developed response to the ideas suggested by the bullet point, and clearly inferred from the text. 3 marks for a detailed and developed response; imaginative, yet clearly drawn from the text. Candidates should write in the mother's voice. (Quotations given here are to support the marker, as candidates must pick up clues, but these are not required in the answer.)
Total		10	

Foundation: Practice Paper 3: *The Adventures of Tom Sawyer*

Section A

1. **d)** Sid is Tom's brother. Tom 'was afraid he might wake Sid' (lines 4–5), implying he sleeps near him and wants to keep his plan secret. (1)

2. **b)** His 'nerves demanded' (line 4) means his instinct is to toss and turn in 'restless impatience' (line 2). (2)

3. **a)** The sound came from the wall, not the hall, Tom believed 'it meant somebody's days were numbered' (line 11): they had only a few days to live. (2)

4. **c)** The reader knows the clock had chimed eleven (line 15) so it must be after that. The night would be over at six o'clock in the morning. (2)

5. To score 2 marks, candidates must explain both words, 'reflections' and 'oppressive', using the definitions provided for support. Candidates should show an understanding that Tom's thoughts became uncomfortable and overwhelming. (2)

6. Correct 'wisht' to 'wish'; correct 'knowed' to 'knew'; correct 'awful solemn' to 'awfully solemn'; correct 'ain't it' to 'isn't it'; remove 'like' or replace it with 'though'. Candidates should correct any of these two mistakes to be awarded 1 mark or four or five mistakes to be awarded 2 marks. (2)

7. **b)** Colloquial verb forms would be used. (2)

8. **c)** Real people, carrying flaming torchlights, are coming towards them. (2)

(Total of 15 marks available)

Section B

Q.	Answer	Mark	Additional guidance
9	*Any two of the following:* 'he heard the clock strike ten' (line 3) – Tom thought it must be daytime and was impatient. 'the ticking of the clock' (lines 6–7) – Tom notices the night-time noises in the dark as time passes slowly for him. 'the clock chimed eleven' (line 15) – Tom was dozing and did not hear it.	4	1 mark for each quotation marking the time. 1 mark for each relevant suggestion of what Tom is doing or thinking.

Foundation and Paper 1 (Reading): Practice Paper Answers

Q.	Answer	Mark	Additional guidance
10			
a)	*Choice of two quotations.*	2	1 mark for each relevant quotation.
b)	*Candidates may refer to some of the following points, when choosing and explaining their chosen two quotations:*	4	Up to 2 marks for exploring and explaining the effect of each quotation/evidence.
	'he lay still and stared into the dark' (line 5) – the eerie mood is created by darkness.		
	'Everything was dismally still.' (line 5) – the eerie mood is created by stillness, with no life around.		
	'Old beams began to crack mysteriously.' (line 7) – old/beams/cracking suggests mysterious sounds around him.		
	'The stairs creaked faintly.' (lines 7–8) – a sound on the stair could suggest an intruder/stranger.		
	'spirits were abroad' (line 8) – the list of sounds builds to create a surrounding mood of unease.		
	'muffled snore issued from Aunt Polly's chamber' (lines 8–9) – Tom's aunt/carer is asleep, in a different room, and so of no comfort.		
	'the tiresome chirping of a cricket that no human ingenuity could locate, began' (lines 9–10) – an irritating hidden sound that cannot be discovered and silenced.		
	'the ghastly ticking of a death-watch in the wall at the bed's head … it meant that somebody's days were numbered' (lines 10–11) – comes at the end of the list of sounds, leaving the reader with the thought that death might be close at hand.		
	'the howl of a far-off dog rose on the night air and was answered by a fainter howl from a remoter distance' (lines 11–12) – even the outside sounds are sinister.		
	The long list of sounds creates and emphasises the eerie atmosphere.		
11	Tom is quiet so neither Sid nor Aunt Polly wake up and discover his escape. (lines 4–5 and lines 8–9)	6	2 marks available for each suggestion:
	Tom escaped through the bedroom window and crawled along the roof, not waking anyone by using the stairs or the door.		Award 1 mark for evidence from the text in own words.
	Huckleberry gave a cat sound (line 16) to let Tom know he was outside waiting. Tom replied with a careful meow, to let Huckleberry know he was on his way.		Award up to 2 marks for relevant explanation of the evidence.
12	'they waited in silence for what seemed a long time' (line 24) – absence of sound and action creates the suspense as we wonder what they are waiting for.	6	Up to 2 marks for each recognition of author's device and explanation.
	'The hooting of a distant owl' (line 24) – onomatopoeia allows the reader to imagine they can hear the eerie call of the owl.		

Foundation: Practice Paper 3: *The Adventures of Tom Sawyer*

Q.	Answer	Mark	Additional guidance
	'was all the sound that troubled the dead stillness' (line 25) – the personification of sound further creates tension of frightening events ahead.		
	or		
	'dead stillness' – in this context 'dead' is used as a metaphor to emphasise how quiet and still the night is.		
	or		
	'dead' – creates and foreshadows a sense of foreboding.		
13	*Huckleberry is the more afraid:*	3	1 mark for recognising that Huckleberry is more afraid.
	He looks to Tom for reassurance:		Up to 2 marks for each piece of supporting evidence/quotation.
	• 'Lord, Tom, they're coming! They're coming, sure. What'll we do?' (line 38)		
	• 'I wish I hadn't come.' (line 40)		
	• 'I'll try to, Tom, but, Lord! I'm all of a shiver.' (line 43)		
	• 'It's devil-fire. Oh, Tom, this is awful.' (line 48)		
	Tom is less afraid and reassures Huckleberry:		
	• 'Oh, don't be afeard.' (line 41)		
	• 'I don't believe they'll bother us.' (line 41)		
Total		25	

Section C

Q.	Answer	Mark	Additional guidance
14	Ideas for the continuation of the story may include:	10	1 mark for a continuation written in the past tense and third-person narrative.
	• *What Tom and Huckleberry see coming towards them:*		Up to 3 marks for developing a response to each of the bullet points:
	• Reward a description of figures, coming through the darkness, in the graveyard, either carrying flaming torchlights, or having lit a fire.		
	• The boys have heard voices, so what they see must be human, spirits or real, and more than one person: 'A muffled sound of voices floated up from the far end of the graveyard.' (lines 45–46)		1 mark for including a straightforward reference to the ideas suggested by the bullet point and inferred from the text.
	• Reference to Hoss Williams may be relevant, whether to his spirit, or a relation or enemy of his: 'Say, Hucky, – do you reckon Hoss Williams hears us talking?' 'O'course he does. Least his spirit does.' (lines 29–30)		2 marks for a more developed response to the ideas suggested by the bullet point, and clearly inferred from the text.
	• *How each boy would react to what he sees:*		
	Huckleberry has been more afraid and looks to Tom for reassurance. Tom is afraid, but is braver and takes more of a lead, and seems more inquisitive.		
	• Huckleberry: 'What is it, Tom?' (line 34)		
	• 'I wish I hadn't come.' (line 40)		
	• Tom: 'Oh, don't be afeard.' (line 41)		
	• '"Look! See there!" whispered Tom. "What is it?"' (line 47)		

Foundation and Paper 1 (Reading): Practice Paper Answers

Q.	Answer	Mark	Additional guidance

	However, they are in this together, and look to each other for comfort:
	
	• 'the two clung together with beating hearts' (line 34)
	• 'The boys bent their heads together and scarcely breathed.' (line 45)
	
	(If dialogue is used, it should be within character – Tom more authoritative, Huckleberry looking up to Tom.)
	
	(Reward development and explanation of ideas that can be inferred clearly from the text.)
	
	• *How their night adventure ends: the outcome/ending is dependent on the previous two paragraphs:*
	
	  • The voices come from the spirit of Hoss Williams and other spirits, carrying/lighting fire and so threaten Tom and Huckleberry with damnation/revenge for their disrespect – the night ends with their regret and fear of the spirits.
	  • Or voices come from the spirit of Hoss Williams and other spirits, carrying fire and giving assistance and kindness to Tom and Huckleberry – the night ends with their relief and possible opportunity for further exciting adventures.
	  • Or the voices are not spirits, but come from local people, carrying torches/lighting a fire and may be friendly or unfriendly – the night may end well for the boys, joining these folk – they may be in trouble with Aunt Polly on their return.
			3 marks for a detailed and developed response; imaginative, yet clearly drawn from the text.
			
			Dialogue, if used, need not be in the same style.
			
			(Quotations given here are to support the marker, as candidates must pick up clues, but these are not required in the answer.)

Total		10	

Paper 1 (Reading): Prose Practice Paper 1: *Educated*

Section A

1. **c)** The fact that Tara lives with her father and her siblings while her grandparents live nearby is clearly stated in the introduction. (1)

2. **a)** Tara is keen to get to her grandmother's house as she 'got into the habit of skipping breakfast' (line 5) and going straight to the barn to do her chores. The verbs give the reader a lot of information quickly about what she did before arriving at her grandmother's house and suggest that she was in a hurry to get there. (2)

3. **d)** This section contains dialogue: '"I wouldn't like it," I said.' (line 10); description of actions: 'She poured the milk and handed me the bowl' (line 12); and thoughts: 'I tried to imagine school but couldn't.' (line 18) (2)

4. **d)** This is an idiom to describe an unstoppable person; the answer is further supported by the adjectives 'impatient, aggressive, self-possessed' (line 24) which Tara uses to describe her grandmother. (2)

5. **c)** It is the painting of 'especially her eyebrows' (line 26) that makes her face seem 'stretched' (line 27) and gives her an 'expression of boredom, almost sarcasm'. (line 28) (2)

6. **c)** She has just made quite an aggressive comment about Tara's father: 'Your dad can't make me do a damned thing.' (line 31) This phrase is used to show that she is bracing herself in a determined way, almost as if he is in the room. (2)

7. **b)** The scheme is well plotted because her grandmother knows that Tara's father has to keep working in the weeks when the weather is not too cold. 'Dad always worked from sunup to sundown in the weeks before the first snow.' (lines 36–37) (2)

8. **a)** Tara is the author of the book and she is writing about her own life in the first person: 'It wasn't long before I began to think …'. (line 4) (2)

(Total of 15 marks available)

Section B

Q.	Answer	Mark	Additional guidance
9 a)	Tara's father believes that to drink milk is sinful (introduction) and her grandmother seems not to support his belief; she deliberately buys a lot of it to oppose him 'Grandma jammed her fridge full of it.' (line 1)	2	Up to 2 marks for understanding why she bought so much milk.
b)	*Suggestions may include:* • She likes milk and her grandmother has a lot of it. • She likes the range of milk her grandmother has. • She doesn't like to think of the milk going to waste.	2	Award 1 mark for each relevant reason given.

Foundation and Paper 1 (Reading): Practice Paper Answers

Q.	Answer	Mark	Additional guidance
	• She likes having breakfast with her grandmother as she has the time to talk to her. • Perhaps she is lonely at home as her father is busy working.		
10	*Answers may include:* Her grandmother takes Tara by surprise as she is eating her cereal: 'How would you like to go to school?' (line 9) – she is not at all prepared for the question. Her grandmother dismisses her statement that she would not like school: '"How do you know?" she barked. "You ain't never tried it."' (line 11) She does not leave any room for discussion. She sat 'directly across' from Tara and watched her closely: '... and watched as I shovelled spoonfuls into my mouth.' (lines 12–13) She is intimidating Tara. She gives Tara no time to think things through: 'Get yourself up real early ... around five ... '. (lines 16 –17) Tara reflects that she can't read and realises she is losing out: at Sunday school 'A boy ... had told all the girls that I couldn't read because I didn't go to school ...'. (lines 19–20) When Tara asks if her father knows about the idea, her grandmother again gives her no room for discussion and has a quick and definite answer: 'No ... we'll be long gone by the time he realizes you're missing.' (line 22) Her grandmother then turns away to shut down the conversation: she 'gazed out the window.' (line 23)	5	**1 mark: general** A straightforward yet relevant response. **2 marks: straightforward** A relevant response, supported with quotation or reference to the text. Or, two relevant points, but without precise textual reference. **3 marks: developed** Two relevant points, linked clearly to the details of the text. Or, one strong point, supported with reference to the text and explained/developed in detail. **4 marks: further developed** Two or three points to develop the response, supported with quotation. An integrated argument; points discussed in combination. **5 marks: insightful** Fulfils all the criteria of 4 marks and draws out deeper implications. Evidence of insightful language analysis.
11 a)	The use of a short sentence 'I didn't sleep that night.' (line 42) creates a tension which reflects the anxiety she feels in her situation. Simple direct statement: She 'sat on the kitchen floor' (line 42) as she was so anxious – she did not even go to bed but was on the floor. The use of time passing: She 'watched the hours tick by' (line 42) – time was going so slowly as she could not sleep. Her eyes were open, aware of every tick of the clock.	4	Award up to 2 marks for each explanation: 1 mark for identifying a relevant detail and for explaining the effect in straightforward but relevant terms. 2 marks for a more insightful and illuminating response.

Paper 1 (Reading): Prose Practice Paper 1: *Educated*

Q.	Answer	Mark	Additional guidance
b)	Incomplete/short sentences 'One A.M. Two. Three.' (lines 42–43) slow the pace right down – time seems to stand still for her as she is unable to sleep; each passing hour seems to drag; it is as if the clock is ticking very slowly. She is worried about going to school as she has never been before: 'I wouldn't like it'. (line 10) She is worried that she cannot read as at her Sunday school 'none of them would talk to me' (line 20) as a boy had told the other children that she could not read. She is worried about what her father thinks of the plan: 'Dad said I can go?' (line 21) She is concerned that her father will want her back/that she will be doing something he will not like 'Won't Dad just make you bring me back?' (line 30) She understands the tension between her grandmother and her father which does not make her situation any easier – she is in the middle of their squabble. She realises that her father must stay and work 'Even if his mother ran off with his youngest child …'. (lines 38–39) She is anxious to do her chores before she goes so that the cows don't escape, 'I'll need to feed the animals before we go' and alert her father. (line 40) She perhaps wishes that she had offered more resistance to the plan. (lines 21 and 29–30) Tara seems comfortable with her life as she lives with her father, does her chores and likes to visit her grandmother – she might feel anxious about leaving this lifestyle behind.	6	**1 mark: general** A straightforward yet relevant response. **2 marks: straightforward** A relevant response, supported with quotation or reference to the text. **3 marks: developed** Two relevant points, linked clearly to the details of the text. Or, one strong point, supported with reference to the text and explained/developed in detail. **4 marks: further developed** Two or three points to develop the response, supported with quotation. An integrated argument; points discussed in combination. **5 marks: insightful** Fulfils all the criteria of 4 marks, but draws out deeper implications. Evidence of insightful language analysis. **6 marks: insightful and sustained**
12	*Answers may include:* Insightful: she understood the tension between her grandmother and her father. When her grandmother bought the milk to drink (against his beliefs) she realised that for her grandmother it was 'an important line to hold'. (line 3) Dutiful: before she went to her grandmother's house she did the chores expected of her: 'I'd slop the pigs and fill the troughs …'. (lines 5–6) Intelligent/understanding/aware of the weather and family behaviours: she knew and had worked out her grandmother's plans to go to Arizona 'but I already knew'. (line 14)	6	**1 mark: general** A straightforward yet relevant response. **2 marks: straightforward** A relevant response, supported with quotation or reference to the text. Or, two relevant points, but without precise textual reference.

Foundation and Paper 1 (Reading): Practice Paper Answers

Q.	Answer	Mark	Additional guidance
	Sensitive/wants to be friendly: she did not like it when a boy at Sunday school teased her and the other girls did not speak to her: 'none of them would talk to me'. (line 20)		**3 marks: developed**
			Two relevant points, linked clearly to the details of the text.
	Loyal: she is worried if she goes against her father's wishes: 'Dad said I can go?' (line 21)		Or, one strong point, supported with reference to the text and explained/developed in detail.
	Observant: she notices details in her grandmother's physical appearance 'especially her eyebrows, which she smeared on each morning in thick, inky arches'. (line 26)		**4 marks: further developed**
			Two or three points to develop the response, supported with quotation.
	Prepared to stand up for herself and her father: 'Won't Dad just make you bring me back?' (line 30)		An integrated argument; points discussed in combination.
			5 marks: insightful
	Wants to do the right thing: 'I'll need to feed the animals before we go.' (line 40)		Fulfils all the criteria of 4 marks but draws out deeper implications.
			Evidence of insightful language analysis.
			6 marks: insightful and sustained
Total		25	

Section C

Q.	Answer	Mark	Additional guidance
13	The table below gives a range of points which candidates may wish to discuss; better candidates will synthesise discussion of more than one point into a paragraph of argument.	10	See mark scheme on page 75.
Total		10	

Point	Explanation	Evidence/Analysis
Tara Westover presents the character of her grandmother through the relationship with her son, Tara's father.	She does not seem prepared to empathise with her son's or Tara's situation or feelings.	'After Dad took up preaching against milk, Grandma jammed her fridge full of it.' (line 1) – she is being deliberately contrary and going against his religious convictions. 'we'll be long gone by the time he realises you're missing' (line 22) – this seems quite heartless.
Although there is no evidence from Tara's father's point of view, the relationship is conveyed as tense, perhaps because of a difference in beliefs.	The rift is so deep that she is resolved to take Tara with her to Arizona, away from her father, siblings and family home.	She is determined to be in control and have things her way: 'Your dad can't make me do a damned thing … if he wants you, he'll have to come get you'. (lines 31–32) She seems unforgiving and angry. When Tara challenges her, she replies assertively, suggesting a deep rift in the relationship with her son.

Paper 1 (Reading): Prose Practice Paper 1: *Educated*

Point	Explanation	Evidence/Analysis
The character of the grandmother is also presented by her physical appearance.	She appears to be an imposing woman.	'Grandma was a force of nature' (line 24) and 'To look at her was to take a step back' (lines 24–25) suggest that she has a big presence in the room.
	She deliberately makes herself look the way she does – perhaps to intimidate or seem younger.	'She dyed her hair black' (line 25) suggests that she wanted to stand out with hair of a very definite colour. Tara calls her features 'severe' which indicates that she is unsmiling and looks strict.
		She uses make-up on her eyebrows: 'She drew them too large and this made her face seem stretched.' (lines 26–27) which she did to accentuate her unusual features.
		Tara describes her expression as one of 'boredom, almost sarcasm' (line 28) which spills over into the reader's understanding of her character.
Her character is further presented through the conversation she has with Tara.	She is direct and straightforward in her questioning.	'How would you like to go to school?' and 'How do you know?' (lines 9 and 11) – her questions are not phrased gently and do not allow Tara time to think and react.
	She is assertive and opinionated in her replies.	'How do you know … You ain't never tried it.' (line 11) – she does not appear to care about Tara's reply.
		'she barked' suggests that her manner is sharp and brusque.
	She is forthright and bossy.	'Get yourself up' and 'Put you in school' (lines 16 and 17) – the imperatives demonstrate a bossiness, that she knows what is best for Tara. She is not giving Tara an alternative.
	She does not care about her son's feelings, perhaps as she thinks he does not put his children first.	'But we'll be long gone by the time he realizes you're missing.' (line 22) – she is quite ruthless in her attitude.
	She has definite ideas.	'You should be in school.' (line 29)
	She shows anger in her response.	'Your dad can't make me do a damned thing.' (line 31) – the swearing denotes anger; she won't be controlled by him, even if he can wield power over her grandchildren.
	She also seems slightly embarrassed at this.	'for a moment looked ashamed' (line 32) – she shows a fleeting self-awareness.
	But … Tara chooses to spend time with her grandmother so she must have some likeable qualities.	'we'll take you with us' (line 17) suggests that her grandmother has a fondness for Tara.

Refer back to page 75 in this section for the full mark scheme for the Reading Paper Section C task.

Foundation and Paper 1 (Reading): Practice Paper Answers

Paper 1 (Reading): Prose Practice Paper 2: *Reckless*

Section A

1   c) Third person narrative, as shown by nouns and pronouns: 'Jacob loved the night. He …' (line 3); lives with his mother and brother: 'his mother's sorrow' (line 6), 'his brother's room' (line 10); no father: 'father's study … his disappearance'. (lines 11–12)   (1)

2   b) He feels he has a pact with the night: 'He felt it on his skin like a promise.' (line 3); and he has no need to be afraid. 'Like a cloak woven from freedom and danger.' (lines 3–4)   (2)

3   a) 'and' joins the two independent clauses to make a compound sentence; 'sorrow' is the abstract noun used.   (2)

4   c) Jacob's mother has 'pills that let her sleep.' in the drawer of her bedside table (line 8); Will, Jacob's brother, 'was afraid of the dark'. (line 10)   (2)

5   d) He reads widely: 'books and magazines' (line 23); he has an interest in planes and making things 'model aeroplanes that hung above the desk' (lines 23–24); he had allowed/ introduced Jacob to share his hobby of models: 'how proud he had once been when his father had allowed him to paint one'. (lines 24–25)   (2)

6   a) The 'sheet of paper slipped out of a book on aircraft propulsion … Symbols and equations, a sketch of a peacock, a sun, two moons … one sentence he read on the reverse side'. (lines 29–32)   (2)

7   d) 'like a shimmering eye,' implies an eye full of life that may be watching; 'glassy' implies the mirror may be made of glass; with an 'abyss' which implies a bottomless gulf beyond.   (2)

8   The mirror will 'open' to show what lies beyond it, for the person who covers his face or who hides his reflection by shielding his face.   (2)

(Total of 15 marks available)

Section B

Q.	Answer	Mark	Additional guidance
9 a)	Mysterious/dangerous/sinister atmosphere	1	1 mark for a straightforward point
b)	Personification/metaphor: 'The night breathed through the apartment' (line 1) suggests the night coming alive, as if the night brings life into the apartment where Jacob lives. Simile: 'like a dark animal' (line 1) adds to the feeling of mysterious night-time life, which is sinister with stealth, and cannot be seen in the darkness.	4	Up to 2 marks for a developed explanation recognising effects of a technique. Up to 4 marks where the candidate recognises more than one technique and develops a synthesised, insightful response.
10	To separate and visually differentiate it from the rest of the text. To add emotion to the text to emphasise how much Jacob wants his father to return.	3	1 mark for each point made. Or up to 3 marks for point/s that are fully developed and insightful.

Paper 1 (Reading): Prose Practice Paper 2: *Reckless*

Q.	Answer	Mark	Additional guidance
	The reader understands it is the thoughts and words in the head of the main character.		
	The additional repetition emphasises Jacob's thoughts.		
	It allows the reader to hear Jacob's voice, thoughts and feelings.		
	They are key moments in the story: in his father's study he feels his father's presence (and absence).		
11	*Clues suggest his departure was a sudden one as the room had not been organised/tidied:* <ul><li>'It still looked as if John Reckless had last sat in his desk chair less than an hour ago' (line 15) – the room looked unchanged, not rearranged for a departure.</li><li>'The sweater he had worn so often hung over the chair' (line 16) – a favourite item of clothing left behind.</li><li>'a used tea bag was desiccating on a plate' (lines 16–17) – his departure was so sudden, he had not had time to throw his rubbish away.</li></ul>	4	**1 mark: general** A straightforward yet relevant response. **2 marks: straightforward** A relevant response, supported with quotation or reference to the text. **3 marks: developed** A developed response, supported with quotations or references to the text. **4 marks: further developed** An integrated response, supported with quotations or references to the text and explained and developed.
12	Jacob feels angry at the situation he finds himself in as he looks out of the window. Metaphor: 'the streets that cut' (line 26) – use of a harsh/violent verb to describe the pattern of the streets below. 'their gleaming path' (line 26) could be added to show clear cut edges of the streets/harsh bright light. Personification: 'windows that punched squares of light into the night' (lines 27–28) – as if an angry person has jabbed holes in the night sky and punctured it.	5	1 mark for identifying a relevant feeling. Up to 2 marks each for identifying and explaining two examples of imagery.
13 a)	*Suggestions may include:* *Jacob's mother*<ul><li>Secretive: 'this was not the first time he had sneaked into the empty room to search for answers she did not want to give' (lines 12–14) – she knows more than she is letting on.</li><li>Unhelpful/unresponsive: she has some knowledge that she does not share, leaving Jacob desperate and unhappy.</li><li>Brave: she has some knowledge, but does not share it, in order to keep her family safe.</li><li>In shock/grieving: 'apartment stale with his mother's sorrow' (lines 5–6) – she is missing her husband.</li><li>She takes 'pills that let her sleep' (line 8) – she is so anxious she cannot sleep without medical aid.</li></ul>	4	**1 mark: general** A straightforward yet relevant response. **2 marks: straightforward** A relevant response, supported with quotation or reference to the text. **3 marks: developed** Two relevant points, linked clearly to the details of the text. Or, one strong point, supported with reference to the text and explained/developed in detail. **4 marks: further developed** An insightful response; two or more points may be discussed in combination.

Foundation and Paper 1 (Reading): Practice Paper Answers

Q.	Answer	Mark	Additional guidance
b)	*Jacob's father, John Reckless* • A man with sinister hobbies: pistols, model planes, books on aircraft propulsion suggest a man who knows how to use a gun and has an interest in planes/flight. • Thoughtless: to leave his family behind, for over a year, with no word of where he is or how he is. He draws Jacob into his world and then disappears.	4	**1 mark: general** A straightforward yet relevant response. **2 marks: straightforward** A relevant response, supported with quotation or reference to the text. **3 marks: developed** Two relevant points, linked clearly to the details of the text. Or, one strong point, supported with reference to the text and explained/developed in detail. **4 marks: further developed** An insightful response; two or more points may be discussed in combination.
Total		25	

Section C

Q.	Answer	Mark	Additional guidance
14	The table below gives a range of points which candidates may wish to discuss; better candidates will synthesise discussion of more than one point into a paragraph of argument	10	See mark scheme on page 75.
Total		10	

Point	Explanation	Evidence/Analysis
Cornelia Funke uses the senses to create mystery with the sounds within the apartment as Jacob moves around.	The sounds of the night, within the apartment that night, establish a mood of mystery. The layering of sounds created, then builds to sustain the feeling of mystery.	'The night breathed through the apartment like a dark animal.' (line 1) – the silent presence of shadowy creature, moving within the apartment, but unseen and unheard. 'The ticking of a clock.' (line 1) uses onomatopoeia to enable the reader to hear what Jacob hears. Written within a short sentence emphasises the sound, marking time. 'The groan of a floorboard as he slipped out of his room.' (lines 1–2) Further onomatopoeia allows the reader to hear the sounds that night. The language choice of 'groan' implies a possible feeling of pain and suffering of well-worn floorboards, as Jacob creeps around again.
	Silence/little sound in the opening section, creates and adds to the suspense.	'All was drowned by its silence.' (line 2) – creates a feeling that apart from the 'ticking' and 'groan' there was an overwhelming silence that night.

Point	Explanation	Evidence/Analysis
The writer further adds to the mood with Jacob's use of touch in his father's study.	As Jacob searches, his desperation grows, trying to find answers that are not there.	'*Come back*! Jacob wrote it with his finger on the fogged up window, on the dusty desk, and on the glass panels of the cabinet' (lines 19–20) – Jacob cannot scream aloud for fear of waking his mother, but the reader feels his desperation by his need to silently voice his feelings using the touch of his finger.
		This action is repeated three times, emphasising his despair at the disappearance of his father. Alliteration in 'finger ... fogged up' and 'dusty desk' pulls these words together and emphasises the neglect in the room.
	His despair grows into frustration and anger, and he lashes out.	'Jacob kicked at the drawers' (lines 21–22) and 'yanked ..., tore down the model aeroplanes ...' (lines 22–23) – use of harsh verbs show that his silent plea went unanswered, and his anger and frustration are building in the actions of his feet and hands.
The use of sight, in Jacob's description of the unusual mirror, deepens the mystery.	Jacob sees the mirror in a new light, with a growing suspicion.	'like a shimmering eye, a glassy abyss' (line 36) suggests that the mirror has a movement that could be watching him with an eerie emptiness beyond.
	As he looks more deeply into the mirror he notices more. He has a growing unease about the circumstances around his father.	'cast back a warped reflection on everything John Reckless had left behind' (lines 36–37) implies a cruel reflection, that life as Jacob knew it was not real.
		'The glass was so uneven' (line 39) adds to the sight of the mirror not being true.
		'darker than other mirrors' (lines 39–40) further adds to the sinister feel.
	The reader feels Jacob's emotions through what he hears, touches and sees with a growing realisation that the life he once led was not what he thought it was. The truth lies in the mystery ahead.	The sight of 'rose tendrils winding ... so real they seemed ready to wilt at any moment' (lines 40–41) – the verbs suggest a life force, pulling and drawing Jacob towards the mirror.

Refer back to page 75 in this section for the full mark scheme for the Reading Paper Section C task.

Foundation and Paper 1 (Reading): Practice Paper Answers

Paper 1 (Reading): Prose Practice Paper 3: *The Shadow of the Wind*

Section A

1. **b)** 'a palace' suggests a fine building; 'carcass' suggests the building is in decay; 'a place of echoes and shadows' suggests it has a sense of mystery. (lines 9–10) (1)

2. **d)** 'He'll be eleven soon, and one day the shop will be his. It's time he knew this place.' (lines 15–16) (2)

3. Daniel's father told him not to tell anyone what he was about to see. Not even his friend Tomas. He was to tell no-one. (2)

4. **c)** Passageways rose to the top in a 'beehive' shape, not descending steeply. (line 22) (2)

5. **b)** Long sentences are slow, descriptive and explanatory about the building; ends with short sentences of action/reaction which highlight and emphasise what has gone before. (2)

6. **a)** Care for the building: 'those of us who know this place' (line 38) implies they know and care for the building; custodians of old books: 'when a book is consigned to oblivion … make sure that it gets here'. (lines 37–38) (2)

7. **c)** Daniel's father brings Daniel to this place: Daniel did not know of its existence and is also stunned into silence by what he sees. (2)

8. **b)** Magic and mystery. Magic: 'sorcery of light'; Mystery: 'the immensity of the place … I nodded, and my father smiled' and Daniel's agreement to keep the secret and to join this new world. (lines 43–44) (2)

(Total of 15 marks available)

Section B

Q.	Answer	Mark	Additional guidance
9 a)	*Suggestions may include:* • 'Night watchmen still lingered in the misty streets' (line 1) • 'as the city awoke' (lines 2–3) • 'like a watercolour slowly coming to life' (line 3) • 'entering a vault of blue haze' (line 4) • 'narrow lane, more of a scar than a street' (line 5) • 'brightness of dawn filtered down … in streaks of slanting light' (lines 6–7) • 'brightness of dawn filtered down … that dissolved before touching the ground' (lines 6–7)	2	1 mark for each relevant quotation, up to a maximum of 2.
b)	'Night watchmen still lingered in the misty streets' (line 1) – effective vocabulary suggesting night passing. 'as the city awoke' (lines 2–3) – personification: effective in showing the city alive with movement, where there had been none before.	4	Up to 2 marks each for exploring and explaining the effects of a technique or short quotation.

Paper 1 (Reading): Prose Practice Paper 3: *The Shadow of the Wind*

Q.	Answer	Mark	Additional guidance
	'like a watercolour slowly coming to life' (line 3) – simile: effective in showing people and activity being added to the mellow lit scene.		
	'entering a vault of blue haze' (line 4) – metaphor: effective in showing a blue misty light ahead which seemed enclosed within the space.		
	'narrow lane, more of a scar than a street' (line 5) – metaphor: the lane has indistinct lines, it may appear smudged and faded, possible sinister connotation.		
	'brightness of dawn filtered down … in streaks of slanting light' (lines 6–7) – alliteration/sibilance: effective as the repeated 's' draws the two words together creating a gentle mood.		
	'brightness of dawn filtered down … that dissolved before touching the ground' (lines 6–7) – metaphor: effective in showing the light disappearing as it hits the ground.		
10	Isaac was not a very big/a short man.	3	1 mark for each point made up to a maximum of 3 marks.
	With a face like a vulture, with a pointed nose.		
	He had bushy/a lot of grey hair around his face.		
	He had a pointed/staring/fixed look in his eyes.		
	He had beady/sharp eyes (blue is incorrect).		
	Evidence based on:		
	• 'A smallish man' (line 13)		
	• 'with vulturine features' (line 13)		
	• 'framed by thick grey hair' (line 13)		
	• 'impenetrable aquiline gaze rested on mine' (line 14)		
11	'Brotherhood': they look like a friendship group or society, joined in a common aim.	4	1 mark for each explanation up to a maximum of 3 marks.
	'Alchemists': they have a look of scientists/magicians.		4 marks for a more developed, insightful answer linked closely to the text.
	'Furtive': they seem to be working in a secret way.		
12	*Answers may include:*	6	**1 mark: general**
	A lover of books:		A straightforward yet relevant response.
	• The role taken from his father, passed to his son, to cherish and recue every book, as 'guardians'. (line 38)		**2 marks: straightforward**
	• 'I will tell you what my father told me, though.' (line 36)		A relevant response, supported with quotation or reference to the text.
	• He owns a secondhand bookshop. (line 40)		Or, two relevant points, but without precise textual reference.

Foundation and Paper 1 (Reading): Practice Paper Answers

Q.	Answer	Mark	Additional guidance
	- He is a member of 'the secondhand booksellers' guild'. (line 27) - His belief in the value of a book and its writer: 'books no longer remembered by anyone, books that are lost in time, live for ever'. (lines 38–39) - 'Now they only have us, Daniel.' (lines 41–42) *Takes his role seriously:* - He wants Daniel to take over from him: 'He'll be eleven soon, and one day the shop will be his. It's time he knew this place.' (lines 15–16) - 'Now they only have us, Daniel.' (lines 41–42) *Good with people:* - Polite to colleagues: '"Good morning, Isaac. This is my son, Daniel," my father announced.' (line 15) - Companiable with his son: 'I looked at my father, stunned. He smiled at me and winked.' (line 23) - 'My father knelt next to me and, with his eyes fixed on mine, addressed me in the hushed voice he reserved for promises and secrets.' (lines 28–30) *Spiritual/believer in mystery:* - 'This is a place of mystery' (line 31) – he believes special things happen here. - 'Every book … has a soul.' (lines 31–32) – he believes in the soul of a book. - 'its spirit grows and strengthens' (lines 33–34) – he believes that a book's essence becomes greater. *Secretive:* - He keeps the secret of the Cemetery of Forgotten Books: 'Daniel, you mustn't tell anyone what you're about to see today.' (line 11) - 'Do you think you'll be able to keep such a secret?' (line 42)		**3 marks: developed** Two relevant points, linked clearly to the details of the text. Or, one strong point, supported with reference to the text and explained/developed in detail. **4 marks: further developed** Two or three points to develop the response, supported with quotations. **5 marks: insightful** Fulfils all the criteria of 4 marks, but draws out deeper implications. **6 marks: insightful and sustained**
13	*Yes:* - Authors of books have put their soul/part of themselves into writing them: 'Every book, every volume you see here, has a soul.' (lines 31–32) 'The soul of the person who wrote it and of those who read it and lived and dreamed with it.' (lines 32–33) - If you believe a book has a soul, it is like a person, and it must be saved: 'those of us who know this place, its guardians, make sure that it gets here'. (lines 37–38) - When you read a book you become involved with it and the author/story it is telling, and the book becomes your friend, which can be re-visited when needed: 'Every book you see here has been someone else's best friend.' (line 41)	6	**1 mark: general** A straightforward yet relevant response. **2 marks: straightforward** A relevant response, supported with quotation or reference to the text. **3 marks: developed** Two relevant points, linked clearly to the details of the text. Or, one strong point, supported with reference to the text and explained/developed in detail.

Paper 1 (Reading): Prose Practice Paper 3: *The Shadow of the Wind*

Q.	Answer	Mark	Additional guidance
	No: • A book is a book, made of card and paper, and it does not have a soul, and so it cannot grow or strengthen as in: 'Every time a book changes hands, every time someone runs his eyes down its pages, its spirit grows and strengthens.' (lines 33–34) • Books do not have a life, they last until they are thrown away/destroyed, so books do not live forever: 'In this place … books live for ever, waiting for the day when they will reach a new readers' hands.' (lines 38–40) • If you buy it, you do own it, books do have an owner: 'but in truth books have no owner'. (lines 40–41) • A book cannot be a friend, only another living thing can be a friend: 'Every book you see here has been someone else's best friend.' (line 41)		**4 marks: further developed** Two or three points to develop the response, supported with quotations that draw out deeper implications possibly considering 'Yes' and 'No'. **5/6 marks: insightful** A sustained response that draws out the deeper insight and implications, showing a clear and full understanding/explanation of 'Yes' and 'No'.
Total		25	

Section C

Q.	Answer	Mark	Additional guidance
14	The table below gives a range of points which candidates may wish to discuss; better candidates will synthesise discussion of more than one point into a paragraph of argument.	10	See mark scheme on page 75.
Total		10	

Point	Explanation	Evidence/Analysis
Carlos Ruiz Zafón writes through the perspective of ten-year-old Daniel. The reader sees the Cemetery of Forgotten Books through his eyes.	As he enters the building, he notices unusual light throughout.	'A blue-tinted gloom obscured the … staircase'. (lines 17–18) This unusual bluish, sad-feeling light greets him, slightly hiding the staircase beyond. A corridor leads him to the hall with 'a spiralling basilica of shadows' that are 'pierced by shafts of light from a high glass dome above us' (lines 20–21). The ceiling is like a church with a glass circular window at the top from which shadows and light curl downwards.
	He is amazed by the immensity and grandeur of unusual and impressive architecture.	'sinuous contours of a marble staircase' (lines 17–18): the adjectives 'sinuous' and 'marble' suggest a twisting outline to a staircase, already with an unusual light, made of a possibly grand, heavy stone.

Foundation and Paper 1 (Reading): Practice Paper Answers

Point	Explanation	Evidence/Analysis
		This staircase has 'a gallery of frescoes peopled with angels and fabulous creatures'. (lines 18–19) The paintings appear grand, almost church-like with unusual animals and angels.
		Even the corridor is 'palatial' (line 19), reminding Daniel of a palace.
		The corridor leads to 'a sprawling round hall' with light and shadows twisting from above. (lines 19–20) This big rambling hall, leading from the corridor, must have appeared imposing and grand to Daniel.
		From the hall 'A labyrinth of passageways and crammed bookshelves rose from base to pinnacle like a beehive'. (lines 21–22) The maze of walkways was packed with books. The simile 'like a beehive' enables the reader to picture Daniel's view of the passages and books, packed intricately together, ready for workers to access books.
		Corridors were 'woven with tunnels, steps, platforms and bridges that presaged an immense library of seemingly impossible geometry'. (lines 22–23) Daniel uses the metaphor 'woven' to describe how the passages of books that form a library link in and out of each other, in a way that seemed hard to believe.
	One thing after another has an impact on him.	Daniel lists everything he sees, in detail, each new piece of information about the architecture adding to and enhancing the last, describing the enormity and magnificence of what he sees.
The writer shows us how Daniel reacts to the building and its people.	As a young boy he is amazed by the building.	The building seems unreal with 'seemingly impossible geometry' (line 23) and Daniel looked at his father 'stunned' (line 23) surprised and shocked at what he had seen, not knowing what to say.
	He is unable to absorb it all and can hardly believe all that he has seen.	'My gaze was lost in the immensity of the place and its sorcery of light.' (line 43) The sheer size and enormity of the building, with its magical light, have left him stunned.
	He meets work colleagues of his father.	He is greeted by Isaac, whose 'impenetrable aquiline gaze rested on mine'. (line 14) Daniel is aware this is a special day, to be introduced to the Cemetery of Forgotten Books, and feels under scrutiny. Strong adjectives 'impenetrable aquiline' imply the lingering look of a bird of prey.
		In addition to the building having a magical quality, to his 'ten-year-old eyes' (lines 27–28) people working there looked 'like a brotherhood of alchemists in furtive study'. (line 28) The simile suggests the workers are also mysterious and magical scientists, working on a secret task.

Paper 1 (Reading): Prose Practice Paper 3: *The Shadow of the Wind*

Point	Explanation	Evidence/Analysis
The way in which Daniel's father speaks to him adds to the importance of the visit.	His father speaks with secrecy.	'Daniel, you mustn't tell anyone what you're about to see today. Not even your friend Tomas. No one.' (lines 11–12) Daniel must understand, this is so important, he cannot even tell his best friend. The imperative verbs show the urgency with which his father speaks to him.
		'Do you think you'll be able to keep such a secret?' (line 42) Daniel is asked if he can keep the secret. The direct question with the use of pronouns emphasises the responsibility being asked of him.
	His father speaks with pride and passion about the place, with the strong feeling of the family heritage.	'Now they only have us, Daniel.' (lines 41–42) tells Daniel the consequence of what he has seen that day.
		'This place was already ancient when my father brought me here for the first time'. (lines 34–35) 'I will tell you what my father told me'. (line 36) His repetition of nouns 'father'/'son' stresses the importance of the family tie and the expectation put on Daniel.
	His father speaks to him directly, in a special tone of voice.	'My father knelt next to me and, with his eyes fixed on mine, addressed me in the hushed voice he reserved for promises and secrets.' (lines 28–30) As his father kneels, to get eye contact with Daniel, his voice changes with a tone of intimacy between them.
	He uses emotive language, with a sense of magic and mystery.	'This is a place of mystery, Daniel, a sanctuary.' (line 31): 'mystery'/'sanctuary' imply secrecy and a safe haven for books.
		A writer's spirit, his 'soul' is 'lived and dreamed' (line 32) by others, would provoke emotion in Daniel.
		A book is 'consigned' to 'oblivion', its 'guardians' ensuring its safety (lines 37–38) would stir up sympathy in Daniel.
		'Every book ... been someone else's best friend.' (line 41) Daniel may relate to a book being like his best friend, Tomas.
	Daniel's father speaks in relatively short sentences.	'Every book you see here has been someone else's best friend.' (line 41) suggests the value he must place on what he has seen.
		'Perhaps as old as the city itself.' (line 35) underlines the importance of the building.
		'Welcome to the Cemetery of Forgotten Books, Daniel.' (line 24) His father is pleased to be able to introduce Daniel to what may be a part of his future.

Refer back to page 75 in this section for the full mark scheme for the Reading Paper Section C task.

Foundation and Paper 1 (Reading): Practice Paper Answers

Paper 1 (Reading): Poetry Practice Paper 1: 'The Choosing'

Section A

1. b) 'Best friends .../a common bond in being cleverest ...'. (lines 7–8) The other answers suggest similarities but not the reason for the friendship. (1)

2. c) The poet has already used 'equal/equally' four times and sees the humour in using the word again (line 8) – to drive home the point. The brackets indicate that the repetition is slightly ridiculous and the humour is recognised. (2)

3. d) The children competed for 'top desk' (line 11) or to 'read aloud the lesson'. (line 12) The narrator had a 'terrible fear' (line 14) about Mary's 'superiority at sums'. (line 15) Up to this point they had been equal at everything. (2)

4. b) The apartment was cheaper ('cheaper rent') (line 23); her father kept greyhounds but it is not known for sure that he raced them; 'He didn't believe in high school education,/especially for girls'. (lines 28–29) (2)

5. c) The early memories are when the girls were in primary school, so she would now be about 18; the narrator is on the bus holding her library books so the inference is that she has been studying there, especially as she is comparing herself to Mary who is no longer at school. (2)

6. a) It is seeing Mary's very different life that triggers her thoughts/story telling: 'Oh, you can see where the attraction lies/in Mary's life'. (lines 40–41) (2)

7. b) The only statement which is completely wrong is that the narrator definitely envies Mary's life. The others are ambiguous: the lines contain mixed messages – she can see the attraction in Mary's life but she does not envy her; 'really' (line 42) suggests that she is trying to persuade herself that she does not envy her or it could be confirming that she does not envy her. (2)

8. c) The narrator is not aware of making choices; the choices were made for her and Mary by others. (2)

(Total of 15 marks available)

Section B

Q.	Answer	Mark	Additional guidance
9 a)	They are both top of the class academically.	3	1 mark each for up to three points made.
	Their hair and ribbons are the same colour.		
	They behave in a similar way – they are both shy/they have nice manners when they receive their prizes.		
	They both feel proud of their achievements.		
b)	*Similarities emphasised through repetition of words/phrases:*	4	Up to 2 marks for each identification and explanation of the effect of repetition.
	• Repetition of 'equal'/'equally' throughout (lines 1, 3, 6, 8) drives home the similarity (and bond) between the girls at school in their appearance, behaviour and academic status.		

Paper 1 (Reading): Poetry Practice Paper 1: 'The Choosing'

Q.	Answer	Mark	Additional guidance
	• Repetition of 'Mary and I' (lines 1 and 7) suggests that they are seen as similar girls/a unit in their friendship. • Repetition of 'we' (lines 1 and 4) suggests that they are seen as good friends, often together, and the narrator views them as a friendship unit. • Repetition of 'coloured' (line 2) emphasises that their appearance was similar/'mouse-coloured' connotes that their behaviour was similarly shy and mouse-like.		
10 a)	Although the girls lived in the same type of house, the people and things within it were different. Their family life, rather than their school life, influenced the different choices made for the girls.	2	1 mark for each relevant point in own words, up to a maximum of 2.
b)	The stanza is short and so stands out. The sentences within it are short and to the point. Use of contrasts: 'the same houses, different homes' (line 18); at school everything was the same for the girls and their houses were similar, but their different homes/families influenced their lives. Oblique reference to the title ('The Choosing') is made for the first time 'where the choices were made' (line 19) – this part of the girls' lives is significant – a turning point. The stanza has a regular rhythm which locks it together and makes it stand out in contrast to most of the rest of the poem. The stanza has a regular rhyme scheme 'stayed'/'made' (lines 17 and 19) 'scheme'/'homes' – half rhyme (lines 16 and 18). This gives the stanza impact/movement and the similar sounds seal it together. The 'I' (line 16) and the 'we' (line 17) lull the reader into thinking that nothing has changed; this gives greater impact to the next two lines.	4	Up to 2 marks each for exploring and explaining the effects of a technique or short quotation.
11 a)	The inference is that Mary's home life and her father's beliefs contrast with the narrator's. They moved to a cheaper home 'three-apartment/and a cheaper rent' (lines 22–23) so the inference is that they did not have as much money as the narrator which might affect life choices. The inference is that Mary's father looks rather dishevelled 'contrasting strangely/with the elegant greyhounds by his side' (lines 26–27) – the greyhounds could be raced for money/betting profits which might be an alien world to the narrator. This emphasises the girls' diverging lives. His ideas about girls' education/school uniform: 'He didn't believe in high school education,/especially for girls,/or in forking out for uniforms.' (lines 28–30) by inference contrasts with the narrator's family's beliefs as she has continued her education. Different life choices are emphasised.	4	1 mark for each relevant yet straightforward point, or up to 2 marks for points which are developed and supported by textual reference.

Foundation and Paper 1 (Reading): Practice Paper Answers

Q.	Answer	Mark	Additional guidance
b)	'I don't know exactly why they moved,/but anyway they went.' (lines 20–21) 'Something about' (line 22) – the narrator does not want to be judgemental as her remarks are deliberately casual and slightly vague. 'I don't know exactly why they moved,/but anyway they went.' (lines 20–21) 'Something about' (line 22) – the narrator is reflective and looking back with hindsight. 'Mary's father, muffled, contrasting strangely/with the elegant greyhounds by his side.' (lines 26–27) – she is not critical but gently suggests what she thinks by the comparison. 'especially for girls' (line 29) – she perhaps thinks that Mary's father's beliefs are understandable in his context/she is not critical. 'forking out for uniforms' (line 30) – by using this colloquial expression she may imply that she agrees with him that uniforms are a waste of money/she is putting herself in his shoes.	4	**1 mark: general** A straightforward yet relevant response. **2 marks: straightforward** A relevant response, supported with quotation or reference to the text. Or, two relevant points, but without precise textual reference. **3 marks: developed** Two relevant points, linked clearly to the details of the text. Or, one strong point, supported with reference to the text and explained/developed in detail. **4 marks: further developed** An insightful response; two or more points may be discussed in combination.
12	'from the library' (lines 32 and 43) – the repetition of this emphasises how differently the girls spend their time. 'sitting near me on the bus' (line 33) – the girls are physically close, but no longer emotionally, as their lives have gone in different directions. 'Mary' (line 34) is on a line of its own; previously it was 'Mary and I' (lines 1 and 7) – emphasising that they are no longer together as friends but have gone their separate ways. 'with a husband who is tall,/curly haired, has eyes/for no one else but Mary' (lines 35–37) – his attractiveness and love for Mary is in contrast to the narrator's solitary state coming from the library and sitting by herself on the bus. Mary's 'arms are round the full-shaped vase/that is her body' (lines 38–39) – a metaphor for her expecting a baby. This is compared to the narrator's arms which are 'full of books' (line 44) – their different lives are symbolised and contrasted through what they are carrying.	4	Up to 2 marks for each identification and exploration of the word pictures.
Total		25	

Paper 1 (Reading): Poetry Practice Paper 1: 'The Choosing'

Section C

Q.	Answer	Mark	Additional guidance
13	The table below gives a range of points which candidates may wish to discuss; better candidates will synthesise discussion of more than one point into a paragraph of argument.	10	See mark scheme on page 75.
Total		10	

Point	Explanation	Evidence/Analysis
Liz Lochhead aids the reader to have a better understanding of the meaning of the poem through the use of stanzas and their changes in focus.	The use of stanzas and changes in focus help the reader to navigate their way through the story and understand its chronological unfolding and the narrator's feelings behind the story. The poet is not restricted to keeping the stanzas the same length, so each part of the story can be told fully and clearly.	The stanzas work like paragraphs for the reader. Each stanza is about a slightly different part of the story. The story unfolds clearly from then to now and includes the narrator's feelings at different points. For example: Stanza 1: contains initial information about the girls' early school lives. Stanza 2: the tone slightly changes as the reader realises that there was some tension/rivalry between the girls shown by 'my terrible fear/of her superiority at sums'. (lines 14–15) Stanza 3: this is a short turning point where the different homes are mentioned and the title is indirectly mentioned in 'the same houses, different homes,/where the choices were made'. (lines 18–19) Stanza 4: the narrator tells of her memories and observations of Mary's father. Stanza 5: the focus switches to the present and what the narrator observes and is thinking now. Stanza 6: the narrator sums up her questioning but comes to no definite answer. The stanzas do not have a regular rhythm and sentence lengths vary. This gives the poet the opportunity to present the story clearly without being restricted by rules of form.
The use of tense change further aids the reader to have a clearer understanding of the meaning of the poem.	The changes of tense provide flashbacks to the past and then bring the focus to the present – the reader therefore is given a fuller picture of events and feelings.	The use of the past tense provides a clear flashback of memories. The first four stanzas are in the past tense: 'We were first equal Mary and I'. (line 1) They clearly provide the reader with the narrator's memories of the girls' school and home lives. In Stanza 5 the tense switches to the present: 'I am coming home from the library'. (line 32) The narrator describes what she sees and it is as if the reader is there with her. She also tells the reader what and how she is thinking and feeling: 'not that I envy her, really'. (line 42) In 'Oh, you can see where the attraction lies' (line 40) the present tense (and use of the pronoun 'you') is used to talk directly with the reader, thus involving them fully in the story and its associated feelings.

Foundation and Paper 1 (Reading): Practice Paper Answers

Point	Explanation	Evidence/Analysis
Both the use of rhyme and non-rhyme provide continuing clarity of meaning for the reader.	*Use of rhyme:* In Stanzas 3 and 6 the rhyme allows the stanzas to stand out and so the reader more readily absorbs their message.	In Stanza 3 the rhyme signals a turning point. There is an ABCB pattern: 'schemes'/'stayed'/'homes'/'made'. (lines 16–19) The lines are sealed together (combined with a regular rhythm) and therefore stand out, especially as they are in a short stanza of their own. The importance of these lines is also confirmed by the oblique reference to the title and the message of the poem: 'the choices'. (line 19) In Stanza 6, 'taking' and 'making' plus the reference to 'the choices', (lines 45– 47) seal these lines together to provide a clear ending message. The rhyme once again signals that the focus here is on the message of the poem.
	Choice of non-rhyme: This allows the poet a freedom with word choices which enables the story and message to be presented clearly. A meaningful and thought-provoking message can be told with an uncontrived simplicity.	The absence of rhyme means that the story can be told as if the narrator is speaking directly to the reader. Natural speech rhythms aid the clarity of the meaning and message: 'I don't know exactly why they moved,/but anyway they went.' (lines 20–21) The general use of non-rhyme means that the key stanzas using rhyme stand out, especially as they hold the main meaning and message.

Refer back to page 75 in this section for the full mark scheme for the Reading Paper Section C task.

Paper 1 (Reading): Poetry Practice Paper 2: 'Sir Gawain and the Green Knight'

Section A

1. c) January 1st as 'night passes and New Year draws near' (line 1), shows it is the end of the night-time and the new year, January 1st, is starting; dawn is shown by 'night passes' (line 1), 'drawing off darkness' (line 2). (2)

2. b) 'Drawing off' implies the darkness of the night is being pulled away, giving way to morning. (2)

3. a) Amongst hills and valleys: 'whistling between hills/ … drifts in the dales' (lines 7–8); windy weather: 'whip-cracking wind … whistling between hills' (line 7), heavy rain: 'clouds decanted their cold rain earthwards' (line 4), snow: 'driving snow' (line 8). (2)

4. c) The crow of the cock signals day has arrived when he is to set off; each 'crow' brings his fate closer. (2)

5. d) He readily brings the armour: '… came quickly,/bounded from his bedsheets, bringing his garments' (lines 15–16); Gawain has already dressed himself: 'Before day had dawned he was up and dressed' (line 12); his servant fastens his outer clothes tightly and 'then his armour' (line 19). The servant has not maintained the armour which had been 'looked after all the while by the household'. (line 19)

   The servant will also saddle his horse: 'To suit him in metal and to saddle his mount/he called for a servant'. (lines 14–15) (2)

6. b) A colon is used to introduce or direct attention to a list. (1)

7. a) Proper noun: 'Greece'; common nouns: 'piece', 'man', 'steed'. (2)

8. c) He feels anxious: 'his lids are lowered but he sleeps very little' (line 10); he is ready: his armour has been polished and prepared by the household 'for which he is grateful/indeed'. (lines 22–23) (2)

(Total of 15 marks available)

Section B

Q.	Answer	Mark	Additional guidance
9 a)	'clouds decanted their cold rain earthwards' (line 4) 'the nithering north needled man's very nature' (line 5) 'creatures were scattered by the stinging sleet' (line 6) 'Then a whip-cracking wind comes whistling between hills' (line 7) 'driving snow into deepening drifts in the dales' (line 8)	2	1 mark for each chosen quotation.
b)	'clouds decanted their cold rain earthwards' (line 4): the metaphor 'decanted' implies clouds pouring out rain onto the earth.	4	Up to 2 marks each for exploring and explaining the effects of quotation/ techniques. Credit candidates who attempt line 5, including 'nithering'.

Foundation and Paper 1 (Reading): Practice Paper Answers

Q.	Answer	Mark	Additional guidance
	'the nithering north needled man's very nature' (line 5): 'nithering' is an old word meaning 'pinched with cold' and can be further understood in context with 'needled' that the weather in the north aggravates and is sharp towards humans. The alliterative 'n' sound pulls the words together, for greater emphasis. 'creatures were scattered by the stinging sleet' (line 6): the metaphor 'scattered' suggests the sleet was so strong, it cruelly tossed animals around. Again, the alliterative 's' sound/sibilance emphasises the harshness of the 'stinging sleet'. 'Then a whip-cracking wind comes whistling between hills' (line 7): metaphor/onomatopoeia 'whip-cracking' allows the reader to hear and feel the sting of the wind. Onomatopoeic 'whistles' allows the reader to hear the wind screeching through the hills. Alliterative 'w' stresses and pulls words together creating the sound of the wind. 'driving snow into deepening drifts in the dales' (line 8): metaphor 'driving' shows the force of the wind pushing the snow into drifts that are deepening, as snow layers on snow. Alliterative explosive 'd' pulls the words together for emphasis.		
10	*Dark:* 'drawing off darkness' (line 2) 'Before day had dawned' (line 12) The darkness outside, with the wild weather, builds the mood of dread for Gawain. The mood shifts without changing setting. *Light:* 'for the room was livened by the light of a lamp' (line 13) The light of the lamp boosts and energises him to get up and dressed and face the day ahead.	6	Up to 3 marks available for each. Up to 2 marks for identifying a relevant quotation and for explaining the effect in straightforward but relevant terms. Up to 3 marks for a more insightful and illuminating response.
11 a)	The stressed syllables usually fall on the repetition of initial consonant sounds, the alliterative words.	1	1 mark for identifying where the stress falls: on the alliteration/ on the consonants/sounds at the beginnings of words.
b)	The use of alliteration focuses the reader's attention on certain words and links them together for greater emphasis. These words evoke a particular mood for that line. Often there are four stressed syllables per line. This emphasises the rhythm and so moves the poem on at speed/always moving towards the next 'beat'. Like a steadily beating drum, it creates tension. It brings structure to the line, giving familiarity.	3	**1 mark: general** A straightforward yet relevant response. **2 marks: straightforward** A relevant straightforward response, supported with quotation. **3 marks: developed** Two relevant points linked to the text or using quotations. Or one strong supported point with explanation and detail.

Paper 1 (Reading): Poetry Practice Paper 2: 'Sir Gawain and the Green Knight'

Q.	Answer	Mark	Additional guidance
12	Line 23: 'indeed.' It links the longer lined section to the shorter lined section. It introduces the next four short, rhymed lines. This is the linking last word of the longer unrhymed section which begins the rhyme for the shorter section: 'indeed' (line 23) rhymes with 'steed'. (line 27) Being on a line on its own and indented, it stresses and adds weight to how grateful he is.	3	**1 mark: general** Identifying that it links or joins the two sections. **Up to 3 marks: developed** Two relevant points, or one strong supported point with explanation and detail.
13	*Line lengths:* Lines 1–22 have long lines. Lines 23–27 have shorter lines. *Rhyme:* Lines 1–22, the longer section is unrhymed. Lines 23–27, the shorter section is rhymed: ABCBA. *Rhythm:* Lines 1–22 have a rhythm, often four stresses per line. Lines 23–27 have a different rhythm, with three stresses per line. *Alliteration:* Lines 1–22 use alliteration freely to create the stresses. Lines 23–27 only once use alliteration.	6	**Up to 2 marks: straightforward** A relevant comparison between the longer and shorter sections. **Up to 4 marks: developed** Two or three points of developed comparison. **Up to 6 marks: insightful** More developed comparisons. Or fulfils the criteria of 4 marks, but draws out detailed analysis.
Total		25	

Section C

Q.	Answer	Mark	Additional guidance
14	The table below gives a range of points which candidates may wish to discuss; better candidates will synthesise discussion of more than one point into a paragraph of argument.	10	See mark scheme on page 75.
Total		10	

Foundation and Paper 1 (Reading): Practice Paper Answers

Point	Explanation	Evidence/Analysis
Sir Gawain's state of mind is influenced by the events of the weather.	*Dread (or similar):* As he lies in bed, sleeping little, in anticipation of the quest ahead, he is all too aware of the difficult weather conditions. This challenging journey adds to the dread of the meeting with the Green Knight. Alliteration and vocabulary choices set a harsh tone and foreshadow the meeting with the knight.	'But wild-looking weather was about in the world' (line 3): the alliterative 'w' sound pulls the words together, emphasising the sound of the wildness, possibly foreshadowing the wildness to come during his quest. 'clouds decanted their cold rain earthwards' (line 4): the metaphor 'decanted' implies clouds pouring out rain onto the earth which would make his journey to the knight much harder. 'the nithering north needled man's very nature' (line 5): 'nithering' is an old word meaning 'pinched with cold' and can be further understood in context with 'needled' that the weather in the north aggravates and is sharp towards humans. The alliterative 'n' sound pulls the words together, giving greater emphasis. This further adds to the difficult and painful journey that lies ahead. 'creatures were scattered by the stinging sleet' (line 6): the metaphor 'scattered' suggests the sleet was so strong, it cruelly tossed animals around. Again, the alliterative 's' sound/sibilance emphasises the 'stinging sleet' and the harshness of the weather. He may dread that, if animals were being tossed around by the weather, then so would he. 'Then a whip-cracking wind comes whistling between hills' (line 7): metaphor/onomatopoeia/alliteration. Sir Gawain can hear the 'whip-cracking wind' and these violent sounds may foreshadow what is to come. Onomatopoeic 'whistles' reminds Sir Gawain how strong the wind is screeching through the hills, and this will be difficult to ride through. Alliterative 'w' emphasises and pulls these words together for greater effect and provides the sound of the wind. 'driving snow into deepening drifts in the dales' (line 8): metaphor 'driving' shows the force of the wind pushing the snow into drifts that are deepening, as snow layers on snow. Alliterative explosive 'd' emphasises and pulls words together. The snow is gathering in the land ahead, making his journey even more difficult. Sir Gawain listens to the weather outside: 'Alert and listening, Gawain lies in his bed' (line 9) considering the effect this will have on his journey.

Paper 1 (Reading): Poetry Practice Paper 2: 'Sir Gawain and the Green Knight'

Point	Explanation	Evidence/Analysis
His state of mind is influenced by the actions of the servants.	*Gratitude (or similar):* Sir Gawain must face the Green Knight alone. But he is very thankful for the willingness of his servant and the helpful actions of the household staff in preparing his armour. Their support gives him encouragement.	Sir Gawain is able to call for his own servant: 'To suit him in his metal and to saddle his mount/he called for a servant, who came quickly'. (lines 14–15) Once up, he must face the day ahead, and the presence of his willing servant who 'came quickly' will be a reassurance for him.
		'bounded from his bedsheets, bringing his garments' (line 16) shows that the servant is eager to be of help. The explosive alliterative 'b' sound in 'bounded' and 'bedsheets' emphasises how quickly and willingly he came to Sir Gawain.
		'He swathes Sir Gawain in glorious style'/first fastening clothes to fend off the frost' (lines 17–18) implies he dressed Sir Gawain with care and pride for the quest, ensuring he would be warm and kitted out properly.
		'then his armour, looked after all the while by the household' (line 19) tells us that, in addition to his servant, the household staff have prepared his armour in readiness.
		'the buffed and burnished stomach and breastplates' (line 20): the alliterative 'b' emphasises how much polishing has gone into the armour that will cover his body. This will give him confidence that he looks well-prepared to his opponent, the knight.
		'and the rings of chain-mail, raked free of rust,/all gleaming good as new' (lines 21–22) further adds to the care the staff have shown, with alliterative 'r' emphasising how they have 'raked' the chain-mail thoroughly, to ensure it is rust free and effective.
		'for which he is grateful/indeed' (lines 22–23): 'indeed' being set in a line of its own, and joining both sections, gains importance, emphasising how he appreciates his servant and the household for their helpful preparations.
His state of mind is influenced by his readiness for action.	*More confident and determined (or similar):* He will present to the knight looking ready for action, in well-prepared armour which will give him confidence and courage.	'With every polished piece/no man shone more,/from here to ancient Greece.' (lines 24–26) The alliteration of the 'p' sound enhances how gleaming he looks. Any opponent of the knight, for many miles around, could not present better than Sir Gawain.
	Now he is as ready as he can be. He calls for his horse.	'He sent then for his steed.' (line 27) This short sentence, with alliterative 's' highlighting those words, emphasises his command that he is ready and determined to go.

Refer back to page 75 in this section for the full mark scheme for the Reading Paper Section C task.

Foundation and Paper 1 (Reading): Practice Paper Answers

Paper 1 (Reading): Poetry Practice Paper 3: From 'Snake'

Section A

1   b) They go there to 'drink there' (line 3) so they both go there for water. (1)

2   d) 'Crack' is a synonym for a 'fissure' (line 8) which was in the wall from which he came. (2)

3   c) There is no one else there. 'Someone' (line 16) is personifying the snake and in this context 'was before me' (line 16) means arrived there first, not literally standing in front of me. (2)

4   d) It is only the gold snakes in Sicily which are venomous. (2)

5   c) The word 'Sicilian' is an adjective to describe something in/from Sicily. Mount Etna is the country's volcano. (2)

6   b) There are no collective nouns in any of the lines. (2)

7   c) 'I felt so honoured' (line 40) and that was why he 'dared not kill him'. (line 37) (2)

8   a) This poem tells a story (a narrative poem) from the poet's point of view and is written in free verse – poetry which does not rhyme or have a regular rhythm. (2)

(Total of 15 marks available)

Section B

Q.	Answer	Mark	Additional guidance
9 a)	*Language choices:* 'trailed', 'rested', 'sipped', 'softly drank', 'silently': verbs and adverbs with long, light, soft sounds. The snake is presented as calm, quiet, slow, moving smoothly. 'yellow-brown slackness' (line 9), 'soft-bellied down' (line 9), 'into his slack long body' (line 14): adjectives with long, soft, unfinished sounds. The snake is presented as physically soft, sinuous, relaxed. 'with his straight mouth'/'through his straight gums' (lines 13–14), 'yellow-brown slackness' (line 9), 'slack long body' (line 14): repetition which slows the pace. The snake is presented as being in quiet control. 'softly drank through his straight gums, into his slack long body,/Silently.' (lines 14–15): alliteration/sibilance. The snake's sliding, slippery, sinuous, fluid movements are emphasised by the use of alliteration/sibilance throughout. It is as if you can hear the sliding, slippery, sinuous movements of the snake because of the repeated onomatopoeic 's' sounds throughout, which make its presence more real.	6	Candidates should identify two or three language choices. Up to 2/3 marks for exploring and explaining the effect of each language choice.

Paper 1 (Reading): Poetry Practice Paper 3: From 'Snake'

Q.	Answer	Mark	Additional guidance
b)	The use of the pronouns 'he' and 'his' (rather than a more general and less impactful 'it'): the snake seems powerful and significant. *Sentence structure:* Longer sentence: the snake has continuous, uninterrupted actions and movements which are emphasised because the stanza is one long sentence which slows the pace. The snake has a calm, ongoing and powerful authority which is suggested by the repeated use of the conjunction 'and' to link its movements and actions. One-word line: the quiet authority of the snake is emphasised by the word 'Silently' (line 15) which is placed on a line of its own.	3	Up to 3 marks for explaining and exploring the effect of sentence structure(s).
10	Repetition: 'from his drinking, as cattle do' and 'as drinking cattle do' (lines 18 and 19): slows the pace down so that the reader wonders what might happen next. Repetition of 'and' to link the list of the snake's actions – slows pace down and creates an aura around his actions, as if he is all-powerful and time has stopped for him. Alliteration: 'flickered his two-forked tongue' (line 20) gives reader a reminder of the snake's venomous potential. Personification and alliteration: 'mused/ a moment' (lines 20–21) suggests the snake has the power to think what to do next and so time seems to stand still. Word layout: 'a moment' placed on its own. (line 21) There is a pause/time stands still/words read slowly as they stand alone/it is a long moment. Sibilance/onomatopoeia/repeated 's' sound: 'and mused/a moment,/And stooped ...' (lines 20–22) enables us to hear the quiet hissing of the snake as it makes its presence known. Repetition: 'earth-brown, earth-golden from the burning bowels/of the earth' (lines 23–24) is a reminder that the snake might be a creature from under the ground and has its own significant place in the scheme of things. 'with Etna smoking' (line 25) presents the backdrop of a terrifying smoking volcano which is a reminder of earthly forces, like the snake. Punctuation: the use of commas within the long sentence creates pauses when the breath is held, for example, 'drank a little more,/Being earth-brown, earth golden ...'. (lines 23–24) Breath is then exhaled at the full stop at the end of the stanza.	6	Two techniques to be explored. 1 mark each time for identifying a relevant technique that builds tension. Plus up to 2 marks for explanations that explore the techniques.

Foundation and Paper 1 (Reading): Practice Paper Answers

Q.	Answer	Mark	Additional guidance
11	*Voice 1:* 'The voice of my education' (line 26) The tone is commanding: 'He must be killed'. (line 27) The tone is reasoned: as 'the gold/are venomous'. (lines 28–29) But also presents the unexpected: 'the black, black snakes are innocent, the gold/are venomous'. (lines 28–29) *Voice 2:* 'voices in me' (line 30) The tone plays on his guilt/is goading/is challenging: 'If you were a man'. (line 30) It is brutal/violent: 'break him now', 'finish him off'. (line 31) It is commanding/forceful: 'You would take a stick and break him now, and finish him off.' (line 31)	4	Up to 2 marks for explaining the tone of each voice, supported by a relevant quotation.
12	*Word choices showing pleasure:* 'confess …' (line 32): he is admitting that he is disobeying the 'voices' in his head telling him to kill the snake, which suggests how much he likes it. 'how I liked him' and 'how glad I was' (lines 32 and 33): repetition of 'how' emphasises statements. 'he had come like a guest' (line 33): although the snake was uninvited, his appearance that day was as pleasurable as if he had been asked to come. 'to drink/at my water-trough' (lines 33–34): indicates pleasure that the snake had chosen his water-trough from which to drink. 'depart peaceful, pacified, and thankless' (line 35): triple of adjectives to suggest that the poet was pleased that he left calmly and satisfied (but without the need to be thankful as if it was his right). 'Into the burning bowels …' (line 36): metaphor/alliteration – the poet seems pleased that after the visit the snake has returned alive to its natural, if dangerous, place in the world where humans can't go.	6	Two word choices to be explored. 1 mark each time for identifying a relevant word choice that shows pleasure. Plus up to 2 marks for explanations that explore the word choices.
Total		25	

Section C

Q.	Answer	Mark	Additional guidance
13	The table below gives a range of points which candidates may wish to discuss; better candidates will synthesise discussion of more than one point into a paragraph of argument.	10	See mark scheme on page XX.
Total		10	

Paper 1 (Reading): Poetry Practice Paper 3: From 'Snake'

Point	Explanation	Evidence/Analysis
At the beginning of the poem, DH Lawrence presents his feelings through his reactions as he tells the story of the arrival of the snake.	He feels surprised to see the snake there first thing in the morning as it is an unexpected visitor.	'A snake came to my water-trough' (line 1) is the first thing he mentions which indicates his surprise. The pronoun 'my' also emphasises his surprise as he feels ownership over the water-trough.
	He feels respectful of the snake.	The repetition in 'must wait, must stand and wait' (line 6) suggests that there is no choice for him but to let the snake drink first as he is respectful of the snake and feels of secondary importance in its presence.
	The snake's visit made an impact on him.	'for there he was at the trough/before me' (lines 6–7): the personifying pronoun 'he' suggests the importance of the snake's arrival to the poet.
In the description of the snake's movements and appearance, the poet continues to present his feelings about the snake to the reader.	The poet notices the movements and appearance of the snake in great detail. He is watching it closely because he feels fascinated and mesmerised by it.	Long slow sounds in the description: 'And trailed his yellow-brown slackness soft-bellied down' (line 9) emphasise the snake's mesmerising presence.
	He acknowledges the relaxed authority of the snake.	In 'He sipped with his straight mouth' (line 13), the use of personification adds importance to the snake; the use of sibilance draws the words together to provide the snake's sound effects.
		The process of drinking is slow: 'Softly drank through his straight gums, into his slack long body'. (line 14)
	By contrast, the poet feels a little uncomfortable under the snake's gaze as the snake seems to be in control.	Cattle have a way of raising their head and staring: 'from his drinking, as cattle do … as drinking cattle do'. (lines 18–19) The repetition emphasises the slow gaze and deliberate movements of the snake, adding to the poet's discomfort.
	In noticing the action and shape of the tongue, the poet reminds himself of the venomous nature of snakes. This adds to his feeling of discomfort.	Personification and alliteration are used in the line 'flickered his two-forked tongue from his lips' (line 20) to emphasise the snake's slow deliberate power.
		The snake 'mused/a moment' (lines 20–21), 'And stooped and drank a little more' (line 22) which suggests that by contrast the snake is not rushed, not frightened at all.
	He feels in awe of the snake: it has a force of its own because of where it lives and where it has come from.	In 'earth-brown, earth-golden from the burning bowels/of the earth' (lines 23–24): the repetition of 'earth' emphasises the importance and power of the snake and the significance of where it has come from. It is part of a bigger force than the poet and from a deep force underground.

Foundation and Paper 1 (Reading): Practice Paper Answers

Point	Explanation	Evidence/Analysis
	He feels in a state of wonderment/reverence because of the link, through language, of the snake with the volcano.	The alliteration and metaphor in 'burning bowels' (line 23) emphasise the depth from which the snake has come and links with the mention of the volcano Etna in line 25.
		In 'the burning bowels/of the earth/ ... with Etna smoking' (lines 23–25) the images of where the snake has come from and the volcano are now linked, so the power of the volcano is transferred to the snake.
The concluding questions the poet asks himself provide the reader with further detail about his feelings towards the snake.	The questions present the poet as feeling in a state of conflict: the voices in his head are telling him to kill the snake but, at the same time, he is intrigued in, mesmerised by and in awe of the snake, and pleased that it visited.	'But must I confess how I liked him' (line 32) indicates that he admits that he likes the snake and is pleased that it came to his water-trough, which makes killing it hard.
		He feels a bond with the snake: 'How glad I was he had come like a guest in quiet, to drink' (line 33); it was as if he had invited the snake to drink quietly at his water-trough.
	The poet is feeling confused and trying to work out what he is thinking and how he is feeling.	The line 'And depart peaceful, pacified, and thankless' (line 35) tells the reader that the snake just leaves quietly: it does no harm so why should he kill it?
	The four questions emphasise the poet's inner conflict as he wrestles with himself.	The use of the question '... Into the burning bowels of this earth?' (line 36) suggests that the poet feels it is right that the snake goes back to where it belongs – deep inside the earth.
		The poet asks three more questions of himself to identify his motivations and feelings: 'Was it cowardice, that I dared not kill him?' (line 37)
		'Was it perversity, that I longed to talk to him?' (line 38)
		'Was it humility, to feel so honoured?/I felt so honoured.' (lines 39–40)
		These rhetorical questions give us an insight into his confused and troubled mind.
	But finally, he feels he has reached a self-understanding and he feels humbled: it was a privilege to have witnessed the event.	At the end of the extract, he asks a question which is then answered in a short statement: 'Was it humility, to feel so honoured?/I felt so honoured.' (lines 39–40) The repetition of words in the question and answer emphasises the poet's conclusion – that he feels humbled.

Refer back to page 75 in this section for the full mark scheme for the Reading Paper Section C task.

Paper 1 (Reading): Drama Practice Paper 1: *Refugee Boy*

Section A

1. b) Comedy – the device of repetition is used: '... to the front room', '... in the front room' (lines 4–9, lines 12–13); 'toilet' (lines 10–11). (2)

2. d) Mr Fitzgerald forgot his wallet was in his coat: '*Alem comes back in ... Mr Fitzgerald's keys and wallet are in his coat.*' (lines 26–27) (1)

3. a) Thankful: 'Dear God we give thanks for this food and for this family' but unhappy: 'please bring my father back to me as soon as possible so I can leave this place. Amen.' (lines 38–39) (2)

4. b) At least one other child had lived with the Fitzgerald's before: 'He settled in much better than Themba.' (line 44) (2)

5. c) Alem has settled well: 'They love him ... it's like he owns the place. He settled in much better than Themba.' (lines 43–44) and he enjoys following his timetable: 'It's great. ... and a timetable that instructs which lessons are where'. (lines 48–49) (2)

6. d) Upset at the joke about Dickens: 'I am not telling you if that's the way you're going to be.' (line 55) (2)

7. c) He has just arrived as he brings his bag in: '*Alem comes back in with his bag*' (line 26); 'Alem: Where shall I put these?' shows he is not familiar with the house/where to put things (line 28); Mr Fitzgerald implies he is new to the household: 'You'll be right at home here, boy. Our luck has changed.' (lines 29–30); Alem's prayer surprises the family. (lines 38–39) (2)

8. c) A child evacuee, escaping civil war, living with a family who will care for him: 'Alem is a 14-year-old boy from Ethiopia/Eritrea sent to England to escape the violent civil war in his home country ... to live with ... a family who will temporarily look after him.' (introduction). '*The foster family: Mr and Mrs Fitzgerald and Ruth and Alem*' (lines 1–2): The Fitzgeralds will care for him. 'Alem: (*in Amharaic*): ... please bring my father back to me ...' (lines 38–39) shows he is not in his own home/with his own family. (2)

(Total of 15 marks available)

Section B

Q.	Answer	Mark	Additional guidance
9 a)	Lines 36–42: Reason for the tension: surprise at Alem saying a prayer and in his own language/Amharaic. How the tension is broken: Mr Fitzgerald does not allow for a pause and speaks straightaway, not wanting Alem to feel awkward or realise he was surprised: 'Right. Right. Siobhan?' (line 40)	4	1 mark for a reason for the tension that is clearly explained plus: **1 mark: general** A straightforward, relevant understanding of how the tension is broken. **2 marks: straightforward** A relevant explanation of how the tension is broken, supported with quotation or reference to the text. **3 marks: developed** A more developed explanation of how the tension is broken, supported with reference to the text or quotation.

Foundation and Paper 1 (Reading): Practice Paper Answers

Q.	Answer	Mark	Additional guidance
b)	But he turns to his wife for support, who changes the subject and hence the mood: 'Yes. Well. Let's eat and then we must talk about court. Was it a good week, Alem?' (lines 41–42) *Lines 50–52:* Reason for the tension: Mr Fitzgerald asks about 'court' (a place where Alem would need to visit to be able to stay in the country) – 'Court. Nobody has told me about court.' (line 50) This is followed by the stage direction '*An awkward pause.*' (line 51) The pause holds the tension, adding impact to the topic about court, which may not be an easy one. How the tension is broken: Ruth this time changes the topic: 'So what did I do at school today? I wrote an essay on Dickens is what I did!' (line 52) bringing the topic on to one that would distract Alem and that he/her parents could join in with.	4	1 mark for a reason for the tension that is clearly explained plus: **1 mark: general** A straightforward, relevant understanding of how the tension is broken. **2 marks: straightforward** A relevant explanation of how the tension is broken, supported with quotation or reference to the text. **3 marks: developed** A more developed explanation of how the tension is broken, supported with reference to the text or quotation.
10	*Alem will be happy with his new life:* Mr Fitzgerald praises him for his help: 'Alem, you star. Alem knew where it was. Look at him.' (line 29) He refers to their house as his home: 'You'll be right at home here, boy.' (lines 29–30) He is thankful for having food to eat, unlike in his war-torn country, and a family to care for him: 'Dear God we give thanks for this food and for this family'. (line 38) He goes to the same school as Ruth, who praises how he has settled, and so has her support: 'They love him. Everyone's like, pleased to see him now. Now it's like he owns the place.' (lines 43–44) He likes and is impressed by the range of subjects at school: 'It's great. I have mathematics, English, sports' (line 48) and seems impressed with the organisation 'and a timetable that instructs which lessons are where and my form is 3C.' (lines 48–49)	5	**1 mark: general** A straightforward yet relevant response. **2 marks: straightforward** A relevant response, supported with quotation or reference to the text. Or, two relevant points, but without precise textual reference. **3 marks: developed** Two relevant points, linked clearly to details of the text. Or, one strong point, supported with reference to the text and explained/developed in detail. **4 marks: integrated** An integrated argument, developed points discussed on both sides 'Yes' but 'No'.

Paper 1 (Reading): Drama Practice Paper 1: *Refugee Boy*

Q.	Answer	Mark	Additional guidance
	Alem may not be happy with his new life: He does not like living in a strange country and with another family and wants his father to come: 'and please bring my father back to me as soon as possible so I can leave this place.' (lines 38–39) Alem prays in his own language before a meal, while the family he is living with do not pray/acknowledge thankfulness for food. There is mention of 'court' (lines 41 and 50): he would rather be in his own country, living happily, but has to go to a court to be able to stay living in the country which is not his own. This may be a cause of tension for him.		**5 marks: insightful** Fulfils all the criteria of 4 marks, including integrated argument, discussed on both sides 'Yes' but 'No' and draws out deeper integrated implications.
11	Mrs Fitzgerald seems to have the upper hand in the relationship and to be more in control of things. Mr Fitzgerald seems reliant on Mrs Fitzgerald, who appears more organised, to help him: 'Mr Fitzgerald: I put it down here. Then I went to the front room. Mrs Fitzgerald: Have you looked in the front room?' (lines 4–5) 'Mrs Fitzgerald: Did you go to the toilet? Mr Fitzgerald: I didn't go to the toilet.' (lines 10–11) Mr Fitzgerald goes to his wife with his problems/worries for comfort and help: 'I've been robbed. Siobhan, I've been robbed.' (line 24) Mrs Fitzgerald: speaks to him in a simple way, and in the first person plural/includes herself, as if he were a child, showing she is the more capable of the two: 'Is that right? Things get lost! A little attention to detail and we wouldn't lose them in the first place, would we now. Anyway, they're not lost, they're just elsewhere.' (lines 31–33) Mr Fitzgerald: turns to his wife when he does not know what to do: 'Right. Right. Siobhan?' (line 40) Mr Fitzgerald accepts this role, is good-natured and wants to please his wife. Mr Fitzgerald is good-natured in his defence: 'Just elsewhere. Having a rest from the owner is what they're doing.' (line 34) Mr Fitzgerald supports his wife and joins in the joke: 'Mrs Fitzgerald: Who the dickens was Dickens? Mr Fitzgerald: Good question. Ruth, who the dickens is Dickens?' (lines 53–54)	6	**1 mark: general** A straightforward yet relevant response. **2 marks: straightforward** A relevant response, supported with quotation or reference to the text. Or, two relevant points, but without precise textual reference. **3 marks: developed** Two relevant points, linked clearly to details of the text. Or, one strong point, supported with reference to the text and explained/developed in detail. **4 marks: integrated** An integrated response, developed points considered for both characters. **5 marks: insightful** Fulfils all the criteria of 4 marks, including integrated response, drawing out deeper integrated implications. **6 marks: insightful and sustained**

Foundation and Paper 1 (Reading): Practice Paper Answers

Q.	Answer	Mark	Additional guidance
12a)	*By the way the Fitzgeralds speak to each other:* Simple/straightforward, using familiar everyday language, in short sentences, that a family would use: 'Mr Fitzgerald: I've looked in the front room.' (line 6) 'Mrs Fitzgerald: Did you go to the toilet?' (line 10) Ruth is quite rude to her father, as a teenager might be, but her mother reprimands her: 'Ruth: When you start losing things it means you're going senile ...' (line 17) 'Mrs Fitzgerald: Is that right, Ruth Fitzgerald?' (line 19) Familiar/gently teasing: 'Mr Fitzgerald: Just elsewhere. Having a rest from the owner is what they're doing. A bit like someone's homework.' (lines 34–35) Family banter/chat: 'Mrs Fitzgerald: Who the dickens was Dickens? Mr Fitzgerald: Good question. Ruth, who the dickens is Dickens?' (lines 53–54)	3	**1 mark: general** A straightforward yet relevant response. **2 marks: straightforward** A relevant response, supported with quotation or reference to the text. Or, two relevant points, but without precise textual reference. **3 marks: developed** Two relevant points, linked clearly to details of the text. Or, one strong point, supported with reference to the text and explained in detail.
b)	*Through the stage setting:* The scene is set in the Fitzgerald's home which depicts a family life. There is a dining table on the set where Alem and the Fitzgeralds sit to eat. '*The foster family.* *The foster family: Mr and Mrs Fitzgerald and Ruth and Alem.* *Dining table.*' (lines 1–3) The characters eat together, showing a typical family event: 'Mrs Fitzgerald: Time for food.' (line 36)	3	**1 mark: general** A straightforward yet relevant response. **2 marks: straightforward** A relevant response, supported with quotation or reference to the text. Or, two relevant points, but without precise textual reference. **3 marks: developed** Two relevant points, linked clearly to details of the text. Or, one strong point, supported with reference to the text and explained in detail.
Total		25	

Section C

Q.	Answer	Mark	Additional guidance
13	The table below gives a range of points which candidates may wish to discuss; better candidates will synthesise discussion of more than one point into a paragraph of argument.	10	See mark scheme on page 75.
Total		10	

Paper 1 (Reading): Drama Practice Paper 1: *Refugee Boy*

Point	Explanation	Evidence/Analysis
The writer uses the characters of Alem and Ruth to highlight the contrast between the two teenagers through their actions.	Alem is helpful when Mr Fitzgerald has lost his wallet and thinks he has been robbed.	Alem is quietly helpful in finding Mr Fitzgerald's wallet: *'Alem comes back in with his bag and Mr Fitzgerald's coat. Mr Fitzgerald's keys and wallet are in his coat.'* (lines 26–27) He sees there is a problem and calmly collects his bag and Mr Fitzgerald's belongings.
		Alem modestly just asks where to put them: 'Where shall I put these?' (line 28)
		Mr Fitzgerald is very pleased to have someone in the household to help him: 'Alem, you star.' (line 29)
	Whereas Ruth appears to do nothing to help find the wallet, only concerned that the photo of herself may be lost.	Ruth's reaction is self-centred: 'That picture of me. Dad!!!' (line 15)
	Before the food is served, Alem prays, thankful for the food he is about to receive. He does not take food on the table, or a family, for granted.	Alem is grateful for food and takes the occasion seriously.
		'Alem clasps his hands together and prays.' (line 37)
	Ruth does nothing as the food is served.	Ruth is used to food arriving at the table and places no importance on its availability; she does not thank her parents for providing and cooking it.
The writer uses the characters of Alem and Ruth to highlight the two differing teenagers through the way they speak to Mr and Mrs Fitzgerald.	Alem addresses Mr Fitzgerald politely/tactfully, as a newcomer might do. When he finds the missing things, he continues in the same respectful tone.	Alem, trying to help, asks Mr Fitzgerald where he may have left his belongings. 'Could you have left them with my bags?' (line 16) When Alem finds them, he politely asks where he should put them. 'Where shall I put these?' (line 28)
	Ruth makes no attempt to find her father's belongings. She only teases him about him becoming senile, perhaps a negative reminder of him growing older.	Ruth is disrespectful to her father.
		'When you start losing things it means you're going senile. Or there's other things on your mind. Other things to sort out.' (lines 17–18) She is almost, unkindly, provoking him about his age and forgetfulness.
		Mr Fitzgerald makes a joke about becoming senile and remembering to 'dribble' (line 22) and rather than reassuring him she will care for him, her reaction, albeit playful banter, is 'Ugh!' (line 23)
	Alem again is respectful when he talks about school.	Alem fills the family in on his feelings about his new school:
		'It's. It's great.' (line 48)
	Whereas Ruth is indignant and does not take the joke about Dickens in her stride and reacts moodily to her parents.	Ruth does not like the joke being against her and is perhaps used to being the centre of attention: 'I am not telling you if that's the way you're going to be.' (line 55) She replies in a sulky way.

Foundation and Paper 1 (Reading): Practice Paper Answers

Point	Explanation	Evidence/Analysis
The writer also uses the characters of Alem and Ruth to highlight the contrast in their attitudes to life.	Alem understands the importance of possessions and money. Ruth seems unconcerned that her father's possessions might be lost.	Alem appreciates the value of things, coming from a country at war, especially a wallet. *'Alem quietly goes out.'* (line 20) and finds the mislaid wallet/belongings.
	There is evidence that Ruth has 'lost' her homework, or not done it, showing little understanding of how lucky she is to attend school, compared to Alem.	Mr Fitzgerald reminds Ruth that sometimes her homework goes astray: 'Just elsewhere. Having a rest from the owner is what they're doing. A bit like someone's homework.' (lines 34–35)
	Alem is appreciative of the range of subjects he has at school and the efficiency of a timetable, and a class to belong to. He seems surprised that all this is offered to him.	Alem responds enthusiastically to how he is getting on at school: 'It's. It's great. I have mathematics, English, sports and a timetable that instructs which lessons are where and my form is 3C.' (lines 48–49)
	Ruth takes her education, and all school has to offer, lightly and for granted.	Ruth is quick to respond to what she did in English. Yet she talks of her lesson using slightly incorrect grammar: 'So what did I do at school today? I wrote an essay on Dickens is what I did!' (line 52) Perhaps she hopes to impress her parents with her knowledge: 'Dickens was a writer who wrote books.' (line 58)

Refer back to page 75 in this section for the full mark scheme for the Reading Paper Section C task.

Paper 1 (Reading): Drama Practice Paper 2: *An Inspector Calls*

Section A

1. d) This is clearly stated in the introduction. (2)
2. a) Gerald, Eric and Sheila all deny knowing Eva's name. (2)
3. b) She was sacked for 'wanting twenty-five shillings a week instead of twenty-two and six'. (line 9) (1)
4. c) He knows that her father, as a factory owner, employs cheap labour. (line 24)
   He did not pay Eva Smith much money (line 9). (2)
5. b) 'She was taken on in a shop ... Milwards' (lines 30–31) as they 'suddenly found themselves short-handed'. (lines 37–38) (2)
6. c) 'It was a nice change from a factory' (line 39) and 'now she felt she was making a good fresh start'. (line 40) It is not known for sure that she liked working with clothes, people or serving people. (2)
7. d) The Inspector says 'that a customer complained about her – and so she had to go'. (line 48) (2)
8. a) This is a moment of tense drama and the playwright wants to make sure that the producer and actors perform it in the way he wishes. (2)

(Total of 15 marks available)

Section B

Q.	Answer	Mark	Additional guidance
9 a)	*Answers may include:* **Birling:** He is ruthless as an employer as he 'sacked' (line 8) Eva Smith for wanting a little more money. He is not generous as an employer as he was not prepared to pay Eva Smith a little more money. He is not prepared to take any responsibility for Eva's situation or his treatment of her: 'Rubbish!' (line 14) He is impersonal as he calls Eva Smith 'this girl' (line 14) instead of giving her a name. **Sheila:** She is sympathetic to Eva Smith: 'I think it was a mean thing to do.' (line 12) She speaks her mind: 'I think it was a mean thing to do.' (line 12) She can understand Eva's situation: 'Perhaps that spoilt everything for her.' (lines 12–13)	6	**1 mark: general** A straightforward yet relevant response. **2 marks: straightforward** A relevant response, supported with quotation or reference to the text. Or, two relevant points, but without precise textual reference. **3 marks: developed** Two relevant points, linked clearly to the details of the text. Or, one strong point, supported with reference to the text and explained/developed in detail. **1 mark: general** A straightforward yet relevant response. **2 marks: straightforward** A relevant response, supported with quotation or reference to the text. Or, two relevant points, but without precise textual reference. **3 marks: developed** Two relevant points, linked clearly to the details of the text. Or, one strong point, supported with reference to the text and explained/developed in detail.

Foundation and Paper 1 (Reading): Practice Paper Answers

Q.	Answer	Mark	Additional guidance
b)	*Their relationship:* It is argumentative/confrontational/quarrelsome/aggressive/combative. Sheila is critical of her father's treatment of Eva when he sacked her: 'I think it was a mean thing to do.' (line 12) Her father responds 'Rubbish!' (line 14) – he totally dismisses her criticism and then changes the subject.	2	Up to 2 marks: A relevant and straightforward response supported with a quotation or reference to the text or a more developed response with two relevant points but not necessarily with textual evidence or quotation.
10	He presents the dire facts in a direct way: 'Both her parents were dead, so that she'd no home to go back to.' (lines 16–17) He makes the listeners aware that she had very little money as Birling had paid her so little: 'she hadn't been able to save much out of what Birling and Company had paid her.' (lines 17–18) This is also to make the family feel guilty and the audience sympathetic to Eva. The repetition of 'no' drives home her hopeless situation: 'no work, no money coming in … no relatives to help her'. (lines 18–19) He uses emotive language to gain sympathy for her plight: 'lonely, half-starved, she was feeling desperate'. (lines 19–20) He presents all the dire facts about her life in a long list-like sentence, so that her dreadful state is emphasised. (lines 18–20) He uses the impersonal and shocking term 'cheap labour' (line 24) to describe girls like Eva. He implies that more people should react like Sheila: 'I've had that notion myself from time to time'. (line 26) He describes her living conditions graphically: 'dingy little back bedrooms' (line 28) and attempts to make his listeners feel guilty.	6	2 marks available for each of three examples: 1 mark for identifying a relevant detail and for explaining the persuasive effect in straightforward but relevant terms. 2 marks for a more insightful and illuminating response.
11	Use of short/incomplete sentences: 'Not doing her work properly?' (line 44) which moves the dialogue on fast. The Inspector repeats the question words to add weight and tension to his answer: 'There was nothing wrong with the way she was doing her work.' (line 45) The use of short stage directions: '(*staring at him, agitated*)' (line 49) – the audience and the other characters clearly see Sheila's state of mind. The use of short questions: 'When was this?' (line 49); 'What – what did this girl look like?' (line 51); 'What's the matter with her?' (line 57) all convey the characters' unease.	5	**1 mark: general** A straightforward yet relevant response. **2 marks: straightforward** A relevant response, supported with quotation or reference to the text or two relevant points, but without precise textual reference.

Paper 1 (Reading): Drama Practice Paper 2: *An Inspector Calls*

Q.	Answer	Mark	Additional guidance
	Sheila's stammer: 'What – what did this girl look like?' (line 51) indicates her nervousness. The detailed stage directions (lines 53–56): there is action with no dialogue while the important events are played out almost in slow motion. The characters and the audience realise the significance of the moment. Sheila's actions: '... *with a little cry, gives a half-stifled sob, and then runs out.*' (lines 54–55) – tension is heightened as she says nothing but her actions indicate her anxiety.		**3 marks: developed** Two relevant points clearly linked to details from the text. Or, one strong point, supported with reference to the text and explained in detail. **4 marks: further developed** Two or three points to develop the response, supported with quotation. An integrated/connected argument; points discussed in combination. **5 marks: insightful** Fulfils all the criteria of 4 marks and draws out deeper implications. Evidence of insightful language analysis.
12	*Answers may include:* 'Why the devil did you want to go upsetting the child like that?' (line 60): he is starting to feel guilty because of Eva Smith's situation and his daughter's reaction to the photograph. He wants to shift the blame and focus onto the Inspector. Sheila is not a child but by using that word he hopes to gain sympathy. 'Well – why – why?' (line 62): he is buying time here. He is blustering and out of his depth. 'Well – if you don't mind – I'll find out first.' (line 64): he is trying to control the situation and put the Inspector back into a secondary role. 'No, leave this to me.' (line 66): he needs to be back in control and in a superior position to the Inspector. 'And a nasty mess you've made of it now, haven't you?' (line 68): he is pointing the finger of blame at the Inspector in an attempt to make him feel guilty. He wants to shift the blame from his own family. Anger is his only way through now. He wants his family to see him back in charge/worthy of some respect as that is what he is used to.	6	**1 mark: general** A straightforward yet relevant response. **2 marks: straightforward** A relevant response, supported with quotation or reference to the text or two relevant points, but without precise textual reference. **3 marks: developed** Two relevant points clearly linked to details from the text. Or, one strong point, supported with reference to the text and explained in detail. **4 marks: further developed or connected** Two or three points to develop the response, supported with quotation. An integrated argument; points discussed in combination. **5 marks: insightful** Fulfils all the criteria of 4 marks and draws out deeper implications. Evidence of insightful language analysis. **6 marks: insightful and sustained**
Total		25	

Foundation and Paper 1 (Reading): Practice Paper Answers

Section C

Q.	Answer	Mark	Additional guidance
13	The table below gives a range of points which candidates may wish to discuss; better candidates will synthesise discussion of more than one point into a paragraph of argument.	10	See mark scheme on page 75.
Total		10	

Point	Explanation	Evidence/Analysis
The playwright, JB Priestley, presents the Inspector as a storyteller to make this scene dramatic and thought-provoking for the audience.	The Inspector knows more about Eva Smith's circumstances than any of the characters and the audience. He gradually reveals more about her as the extract unfolds. The audience reacts emotionally to the events in her life because of the way the Inspector tells the story.	First, he informs the characters and audience that she worked for Mr Birling but was 'sacked' (line 8) for wanting a little more money. This seems shocking and the audience feels sympathy towards her and outrage towards Mr Birling. He then outlines Eva's dire circumstances when she was out of work with no family support. He does this dramatically, using emotive language to emphasise her situation: she was 'lonely, half-starved, she was feeling desperate'. (lines 19–20) The audience's sympathy towards this girl's story is heightened. He continues to tell how she found a new job and was in a better situation. 'It seems she liked working there.' (lines 38–39) He asks his listeners to empathise with her: 'You can imagine how she felt.' (line 40) Relief is felt by the audience at this point. Dramatic interest is further heightened when he shows Sheila a photograph which she obviously recognises. This is done silently but is still part of the storytelling as he is again in possession of more information (this time a photo) than anyone else.
Dramatic and thought-provoking interest is further maintained because of the way the other characters react to Eva's story.	Eric seems a little sympathetic towards her. Gerald is silent at this point so the audience does not know how he is feeling unless he shows his reaction through non-verbal signals. By contrast Sheila reacts far more forcefully and sympathetically.	The Inspector informs his listeners that after she was sacked 'she stopped being Eva Smith' (line 10) and changed her name. Eric's short response 'Can't blame her' (line 11) indicates that he is listening and seems to care about her but in a rather off-hand way. After hearing about the sacking, she turns on her father: 'I think it was a mean thing to do.' (line 12) After hearing about Eva's dire circumstances, she feels empathy for her: 'I should think so. It's a rotten shame.' (line 21) The stage directions instruct her to say this '*warmly*' – she feels quite passionate about Eva's situation.

Paper 1 (Reading): Drama Practice Paper 2: *An Inspector Calls*

Point	Explanation	Evidence/Analysis
	As the Inspector reveals the reason why she was dismissed, Sheila's demeanour changes.	Sheila objects to the girls impersonally being called 'cheap labour' (line 25) and replies 'they're *people*'. (line 25)
		Unlike the other characters Sheila is keen to hear more of the story: 'But what happened to her then?' (line 29) She shows by far the most sympathy and interest.
		Sheila is '*agitated*' (line 49), asks questions 'When was this?' (line 49) and stammers 'What – what did this girl look like?' (line 51)
		She is now in a state of confusion which is dramatic and thought-provoking for the audience.
	Her questions allow the Inspector to continue his storytelling.	When she is shown the photograph by the Inspector her reaction is intense: she does not speak, but gives '*a little cry … gives a half-stifled sob, and then runs out*'. (lines 54–55)
		The audience now has many unanswered questions to consider.
		It is ironic that Shelia seems to be in some way guilty whereas previously she has been sympathetic towards Eva.
	In sharp contrast with his daughter, Birling's reactions to Eva's story are unsympathetic.	He dismisses his daughter's criticism of his treatment of Eva as 'Rubbish!' (line 14)
		He calls her 'this girl' (line 14) instead of using her name which suggests disinterest and rudeness.
		He makes the assumption that the fault was hers when she lost her job: 'Not doing her work properly?' (line 44) and 'There must have been something wrong.' (line 47)
	The characters' contrasting reactions are interesting dramatically and prompt the audience to think about their roles in the crime, just as the Inspector is doing.	After Sheila's reaction to the photograph, Birling attempts to control the situation: 'Well – if you don't mind – I'll find out first.' (line 64) and tries to shift the blame and focus onto the Inspector: 'And a nasty mess you've made of it now, haven't you?' (line 68)
The Inspector provides dramatic and thought-provoking interest through his comments about Eva Smith's life as a working girl.	The context is 1912 when a woman's place in society and the workplace was very different to today.	The Inspector implies that Mr Birling sacked Eva unnecessarily: 'for wanting twenty-five shillings a week instead of twenty-two and six'. (line 9) He wants the audience to know how little she was paid as a young girl.
	Priestley uses the story of Eva Smith to express his own feelings about the treatment of women. He hopes that the audience will be shocked by the Inspector's comments but will have a better awareness.	The Inspector informs Gerald that she changed her name after the sacking. 'Perhaps she'd had enough of it.' (line 10) He wants the audience to think it out for themselves why she changed her name.

Foundation and Paper 1 (Reading): Practice Paper Answers

Point	Explanation	Evidence/Analysis
		He paints an appalling and shocking picture of her life after she was sacked. It was so bad that she was 'half-starved, she was feeling desperate'. (lines 19–20) This is not just for the benefit of the characters on stage but to open the eyes of the audience too.
		His dry response to Sheila's comment 'they're *people*' (line 25) is to encourage the characters and the audience to think about similar women's dreadful situations: 'I've thought it would do us all a bit of good if sometimes we tried to put ourselves in the place of these young women …' (lines 26–28) He is encouraging a more sympathetic response; he uses the pronoun 'we' to soften his words by including himself in the reprimand.
	As a poor and young girl, Eva was at the mercy of the opinion of her employer and a wealthy customer.	Her life dramatically improves when she gets the job at Milwards. The Inspector believes it was unfair that she was asked to leave when a customer complained about her, especially as 'They admitted that' 'there was nothing wrong with the way she was doing her work'. (lines 45–46)

Refer back to page 75 in this section for the full mark scheme for the Reading Paper Section C task.

Paper 1 (Reading): Drama Practice Paper 3: *Forty Years On*

Section A

1. **b)** She is polite when she offers him a drink, she understands how he must be feeling about retiring and she is supportive when she suggests that Mr Franklin will be unable to cope without him. (1)

2. **c)** This is a metaphor and means to pass responsibility on to somebody else. (2)

3. **d)** The phrase 'within striking distance of the boys' (line 7) has two meanings: to be close by and to be close enough to strike (he later refers to corporal punishment – still used in schools in 1958). The double meaning is used for comic effect. (2)

4. **a)** 'Nonplussed' means surprised and confused. He feels this as he was not expecting those boys to reply to him. (2)

5. **c)** Impudent means cheeky, rude or disrespectful; a charade is a type of performance usually played as a game. It can also mean that the performance is slightly ridiculous – like a farce. This is the only response which covers all these meanings. (2)

6. **b)** Franklin says that they are trying to 'shed the burden of the past'. (line 32) The Headmaster believes that the past must not be shed and that memories 'are garlands' that might indicate victories or celebrations. (line 34) (2)

7. To be in charge is a heavy responsibility (or similar). (2)

8. **b)** Franklin has just plotted to get the Headmaster out of the way. This apparently innocuous reply is sarcastic as he knows they will manage better without him. (2)

(Total of 15 marks available)

Section B

Q.	Answer	Mark	Additional guidance
9	*Through two metaphors:* 'A chance to take up the slack of the mind': as he won't be so busy in retirement he will have the time to explore new things. The 'slack' in a rope is when it is not pulled tight – there is excess rope for the task. His mind will have that similar extra space when he is retired. 'A chance to ... savour the rich broth of a lifetime's experience': he will have the time to reflect and enjoy ('savour'), looking back over his many and varied life experiences ('rich broth'). He compares retirement to having the time to enjoy slowly tasting a hearty and delicious soup.	5	1 mark for recognising the technique. **2 marks for each metaphor:** 1 mark for quoting the metaphor and for explaining the effect in straightforward but relevant terms. 2 marks for a more insightful and illuminating response.

Foundation and Paper 1 (Reading): Practice Paper Answers

Q.	Answer	Mark	Additional guidance
10	The information revealed about the Headmaster as a teacher is indirect: it is through his implied criticism of how Franklin will run the school differently when he takes over. As he says that Franklin will abolish them, it can be assumed that the Headmaster believes in corporal (physical) punishment, games lessons which are compulsory and the cadet corps. He clearly likes the school to be run with strict rules in place. He calls Franklin 'liberal' (line 12) which indicates that the Headmaster knows that he is not so open-minded and that he prefers a stricter regime. All boys follow the same strict regime under his leadership: he thinks that teachers like Franklin are on the side of boys who are not robust ('sensitive'), wanting to keep them happy. He thinks that such boys are never going to be happy so does not see the point of adapting rules for them: 'In my experience sensitive boys are never happy anyway'. (lines 13–14) He is not empathetic. His approach is that one rule fits all.	4	**1 mark: general** A relevant, straightforward response. **2 marks: straightforward** A relevant response, linked closely to the text. Or, two relevant points, but without textual reference. **3 marks: developed** Two relevant points clearly linked to details from the text. Or, one strong point, supported with reference to the text and explained in detail. **4 marks: further developed** An insightful response; two or more points may be discussed in combination.
11	The stage directions suggest a comic moment: the boys are wearing '*gas masks*', are '*larking about*' and '*running at each other like bulls*'. (lines 15–16) This in itself is a funny picture. He '*peers in through the talc*' (line 16) implies that the Headmaster finds it difficult to see who they are – again a comic moment especially as he is in charge. He thinks he knows who they are and calls their names: 'Skinner! Tupper!' (line 17) – but it is not those boys. The actual boys called Skinner and Tupper are messing about in the gallery and '*stand up guiltily*' (line 19) and reply 'Here, Sir!' (line 20) when they hear their names. All combined, this has the comic effect of a farce – where things become out of control and ridiculous. The confusion on the Headmaster's face is a comic moment; he is '*nonplussed*' (line 21) as he does not know what is going on. 'I know those ears. Filthy!' (line 22) is a comic moment as it is an unusual way to recognise who the boys are, combined with the fact that he realises whose ears they are because they are dirty.	4	**1 mark: general** A straightforward yet relevant response. **2 marks: straightforward** A relevant response, linked closely to the text. **3 marks: developed** Two relevant points clearly linked to details from the text. Or, one strong point, supported with reference to the text and explained in detail. **4 marks: further developed** An insightful response; two or more points may be discussed in combination.
12 a)	Franklin is to take over as Head when the Headmaster retires and they both know that he will run the school in a very different way: Franklin is more 'liberal' as a teacher.	2	1 mark: A relevant, straightforward response without textual reference.

Paper 1 (Reading): Drama Practice Paper 3: *Forty Years On*

Q.	Answer	Mark	Additional guidance
b)	The Headmaster thinks that the past should be embraced not ignored; that memories are 'garlands'. (line 34) Franklin wants to 'look to the future'. (line 35) 'Would it be impossibly naïve and old-fashioned of me ...?' (line 30): the wording of his question is teasing/sarcastic which suggests tension between him and Franklin. The Headmaster calls the play (of which Franklin is partly in charge) an 'impudent charade' – which suggests that he is critical of it, thinks it is rude/not appropriate for his retirement celebration. '… we are trying to shed the burden of the past' (line 32) goads the Headmaster as he will soon be the past. He is insulting the Headmaster in a disguised way. 'Shed it? Why must we shed it?' (line 33): he asks questions in response using and repeating Franklin's words as a deliberate challenge. 'Memories are not shackles, Franklin, they are garlands.' (lines 33–34): the Headmaster makes a clear statement and tries to emphasise his authority by addressing Franklin by his name. 'We're too tied to the past.' (line 35) Franklin continues his argument which further insults the Headmaster indirectly. He speaks authoritatively in short sentences. Franklin tries to outwit the Headmaster with wordplay/riddles: 'The future comes before the past.' (lines 35–36) He may choose to verge on impudence here in response to the Headmaster's earlier accusation. 'Nonsense.' (line 37): the Headmaster dismisses Franklin's point of view. Treats him as his inferior.	4	2 marks: A relevant, straightforward response which shows an understanding of their different approaches and is linked clearly to the text. **1 mark: general** A straightforward yet relevant response. **2 marks: straightforward** A relevant response, supported with quotation or reference to the text. Or a more developed response including two relevant points but without textual reference or quotation. **3 marks: developed** Two relevant points clearly linked to details from the text. Or, one strong point, supported with reference to the text and explained in detail. **4 marks: further developed** An insightful response; two or more points may be discussed in combination.
13	*Answers might include:* His command, experience and advice to Franklin evokes a feeling of admiration in the audience: 'It's very easy to be daring and outspoken, Franklin, but once you're at the helm the impetus will pass' (lines 45–46) – he suggests that it is easy to be critical when you are not in charge. The audience might be impressed: after the previous lines where Franklin was goading the Headmaster, he is seen here as in control and is passing on his wisdom.	6	**1 mark: general** A straightforward yet relevant response. **2 marks: straightforward** A relevant response, where the feeling is supported with quotation or reference to the text or two relevant feelings but without precise textual reference. **3 marks: developed** Two relevant feelings, linked clearly to the text or one strong point/feeling supported with reference to the text and explained in detail.

Foundation and Paper 1 (Reading): Practice Paper Answers

Q.	Answer	Mark	Additional guidance
	The audience might feel sympathy for him in his role as Headmaster – it is not easy to be the one in charge: 'once you're at the helm the impetus will pass.' (lines 45–46); 'Authority is a leaden cope.' (line 46) He might be further admired when his experience, which he shares, is greater than Franklin's; he also understands his successor: 'You will be left behind, however daring and outspoken you are.' (lines 46–47) He continues to explain to Franklin what will happen to him once he is in charge. The audience recognises his honesty and admires him for it: 'You will be left behind, just as I have been left behind.' (line 47) His acceptance of his situation evokes sympathy. The repeated phrase: 'you will be left behind' (lines 46 and 47) could invoke a feeling in the audience that he is unnecessarily goading and rude, not just advising, to Franklin. Further sympathy is evoked in response to: 'Though when you fall as far behind as I have, you become a character.' (lines 47–48) – he recognises his own idiosyncrasies which might be even humorous. His honesty draws the audience towards him almost fondly. The audience acknowledges his proud role as Headmaster when he says: 'While I have been Headmaster, Albion House has always been a going concern.' (lines 49–50) The audience feels sympathy for him as after all these years he cannot be sure that the school will continue to be a success: 'Whether that will continue I am not sure.' (line 50) The audience might enjoy his rallying challenge to Franklin: 'It depends on you, Franklin.' (lines 50–51) The audience feels pity for him and sad that after all these years he says with honesty that he is 'not sure of anything nowadays'. (line 51) This pity is further compounded when he says: 'I am lost. I am adrift.' (line 51) The short sentences dramatically evoke pathos. The audience feels sad for him as he seems old-fashioned and out of touch: 'Everywhere one looks, decadence.' (lines 51–52) Finally, the audience might ridicule him when he says: 'I saw a bishop with a moustache the other day.' (line 52) His speech collapses into something comic to stop it being too sentimental. Alternatively, the audience might feel generally relieved that he is retiring as he has shown that he is stuck in the past and his teaching methods do not take individuals into account.		**4 marks: further developed** Two or three feelings, supported with quotations or an integrated argument where points may be discussed in combination. **5 marks: insightful** Fulfils all the criteria of 4 marks but draws out deeper understanding of feelings with evidence of insightful language analysis. **6 marks: insightful and sustained**

Paper 1 (Reading): Drama Practice Paper 3: *Forty Years On*

Section C

Q.	Answer	Mark	Additional guidance
14	The table below gives a range of points which candidates may wish to discuss; better candidates will synthesise discussion of more than one point into a paragraph of argument.	10	See mark scheme on page 75.
Total		10	

Point	Explanation	Evidence/Analysis
The playwright, Alan Bennett, presents the Headmaster's view of himself as a teacher through what he says.	He feels proud of his long time as Headmaster.	When he retires he will 'savour the rich broth of a lifetime's experience'. (line 6) This suggests that he views his time as Headmaster as rewarding and full.
	He is confident that his methods are good ones.	'While I have been Headmaster, Albion House has always been a going concern.' (lines 49–50)
		He calls Franklin 'liberal' (line 12) compared to himself, indicating that he prefers strict methods of discipline.
	He is confident that one rule for all is the right approach.	He likes to treat all children in the same way and cannot see the point of changing the methods of discipline to suit individuals – even the sensitive ones: 'sensitive boys are never happy anyway, so what is the point?' (line 14)
	He thinks that lessons should be learnt from the past – not disregarded.	'Memories are not shackles, Franklin, they are garlands.' (lines 33–34) He thinks that the past and memories are not there to inhibit new ideas ('shackles') but should embellish ('garlands') and improve the future.
	He acknowledges that it is hard to always be in a position of authority.	'Authority is a leaden cope.' (line 46)
		It is as if having the authority is not easy and weighs him down.
	He recognises with honesty that it is time for him to go now.	'… I have been left behind.' (line 47)
		'I am lost. I am adrift.' (line 51): he accepts that he should retire now and make way for someone younger. He cannot keep up any more.
However, in contrast, the audience at times has a different opinion of the Headmaster due to his interactions with the boys and Franklin.	In dealing with the boys, he appears not to be in control and therefore slightly ridiculous.	He reprimands the wrong boys for playing around with the gas masks.
		Those wrongly accused boys then '*stand up guiltily*' (line 19) which adds to the amusement at the Headmaster's expense.
	This is compounded for the audience when Franklin undermines the Headmaster's punishment of the boys.	The Headmaster has told the boys to 'stay like that … until I tell you to take them off.' (lines 22–23)
		Franklin reverses the order concerning the gas masks: 'If you don't get those gas masks off in three seconds flat, you'll be wearing them all night.' (lines 27–28)

Foundation and Paper 1 (Reading): Practice Paper Answers

Point	Explanation	Evidence/Analysis
	Franklin's goading apology to the Headmaster only serves to emphasise and highlight the undermining of the Headmaster's authority.	Whether Franklin means to do this or not, the effect on the audience is that the Headmaster looks foolish.
		'Sorry Headmaster, did I balk you of your prey?' (lines 28–29)
		The word 'prey' influences the audience into thinking that the Headmaster's motivations are not kind ones. Franklin infers that it is as if the Headmaster is like an animal fighting over its vulnerable victim/prey and he steps in to save them.
The audience's view of the Headmaster is further developed because of his interactions with Matron and Franklin.	The Headmaster is made to look doubly foolish in front of the audience: not only do Franklin and Matron trick him but he fails to realise that he has been tricked.	At the beginning of the extract, Matron appears to be courteous and understanding towards the Headmaster. But here it is obvious that this was just an act as she and Franklin have been plotting to get him out of the way.
		'See if you can get the Old Man out of the way …' (line 53): Franklin implies that the Headmaster is useless now by calling him an 'Old Man'.
		Matron is quick to comply with the trick: 'Headmaster, I wonder if you'd come up to the San to have a look at Dishforth?' (line 55)
		The Headmaster cannot refuse to attend to a sick child.
	At this point he seems a pathetic and lonely figure to the audience, in contrast with how he views himself.	'Can I be spared?' (line 57) shows that he does not realise that he has been tricked. This is a pathetic moment added to by Franklin's sarcastic comment: 'I think we'll just about manage.' (line 58)
	The Headmaster is never given a name.	'Sorry Headmaster, did I balk you of your prey?' (lines 28–29): Franklin and the other members of staff always call him Headmaster which implies that he is defined by his role. This emphasises the sadness as he is about to lose that role.

Refer back to page 75 in this section for the full mark scheme for the Reading Paper Section C task.

Paper 2: Writing Practice Paper Answers

Guidance for students, teachers and parents

This section aims to help you mark responses to the practice papers with confidence.

There are two ISEB writing task mark schemes for each essay: the first based on ideas, structure, form and voice; the second based on spelling, punctuation, grammar and expression.

We have included these ISEB grids below together with guidelines to aid the interpretation of the key words in the mark bands. The marking of writing is naturally more subjective than the marking of comprehension answers, but these grids provide a guide to the allocation of marks.

Task 1 is allocated 15 marks for 'Ideas, structure, form and voice' and 10 marks for 'SPAG and expression', totalling 25 marks. Task 2 is the same. Combined they give a total of 50 marks.

The first mark scheme, 'Ideas, structure, form and voice' shows the necessary skills needed in a graded banding system and is explained below.

Read through the mark bands, from 1–6 and this will show you how to improve your writing.

Additionally, you will find some annotated sample essay answers, with plans which provide further support.

Paper 2: ISEB writing task mark scheme – Ideas, structure, form and voice

Ideas, structure, form and voice		15 marks per task (Total 30)
Band	Mark	Descriptors
6	14–15	• precise and imaginative use of **prompts** • intuitive use of appropriate **features of form** • **achieves the given purpose** with flair and in detail • **structured** masterfully to achieve appropriate effects • sustained use of an appropriate **register**; choice of **voice** and **perspective** to engage reader
5	12–13	• precise and interesting use of **prompts** • careful employment of appropriate **features of form** • **achieves the purpose** effectively and in some detail • logical and appropriate **structure**; good sequencing and use of paragraphs • consistent use of appropriate **register**; appropriate use of **perspective** and **voice**
4	10–11	• a little licence taken with **prompts**/or clear use of prompts, but uninspired • some use of appropriate **features of form** • mostly **achieves the purpose**; an attempt to include detail • an attempt to **structure** the writing logically, which may not be sustained; some effective paragraphing • an attempt to use an appropriate **register**, to take a relevant **perspective** and/or **voice**

Paper 2: Writing Practice Paper Answers

Band	Mark	Descriptors
3	8–9	• the response strays from the **prompts**
		• there is little evidence of appropriate **features of form**
		• partly **achieves the purpose**; ideas may be general or vague
		• **structure** is unclear or largely unsustained
		• little attempt to adopt an appropriate **register**; no evident consideration of **perspective** or **voice**
2	6–7	• response lacks relevance to the chosen task; writing is too vague or lacking in relevance to **achieve the purpose**
		• no evident consideration of **form** or **structure**
		• **register**, **voice** and **perspective** are not appropriate or relevant to the purpose and form of writing
1	1–5	• an attempt to respond

Help with interpreting key words in the mark scheme

As you mark your responses to the practice paper writing tasks, check that you have addressed the points in **bold** above and included the features specified below.

Ideas, form and purpose

Prompts: the essay must be relevant and based on the given title with appropriate reference to it. There may also be prompts within the title – these are very helpful so follow them.

Underline the key words in the tasks so that you are sure that you are choosing and responding to the prompts and using the correct style of writing: narrative, descriptive, informative, discursive, persuasive.

Be certain that you have enough ideas to write the essay: they should be thought-provoking, engaging and, if relevant, informative and original.

Features of form: form means the type of writing you are asked to do. For example: story; description; news report; report or study drawing conclusions; information pamphlet; blog post; informing of an issue and making recommendations; speech or debate; letter of complaint or recommendation.

Make sure you employ the appropriate form for your essay.

Achieves the purpose: the purpose of the writing should be understood. What is its point? Are you entertaining, informing, explaining, advising, discussing, persuading? Take notice, also, whether there is a reader ('audience') other than your examiner as in, for example, a letter to your headteacher.

To deliver both the form and its purpose strongly, these pointers might be helpful:

Fiction

Check that you have enough suitable ideas to sustain the writing, particularly if you choose the description.

Check your ideas are not over-ambitious or complicated for the time allowed.

A range of writing features such as imagery, sound devices and the powerful use of vocabulary should be used to enhance the composition and engage and entertain the reader. It is also worth remembering that this is an exam task and so aim to show a range of writing techniques. These should be particularly evident in descriptive writing.

See samples later in this section for further guidance.

Guidance for students, teachers and parents

Story

The ability to focus on, and write with, sufficient detail will engage the reader and ensure that the writing is not mainly 'plot driven'.

Readers need to be able to picture their surroundings: appropriate setting details may range from the overview, such as weather and light, to the immediate foreground.

To provide this detail, the setting(s) could be explored through a variety of senses.

Characters should be developed in a detailed way to go beyond physical attributes and to include consistent and believable actions, dialogue, reactions and feelings. Care should be taken not to overuse dialogue.

Description

Generally, the detail should be greatly enhanced.

Of a place: readers need to be able to picture their surroundings: appropriate setting details may range from the overview, such as weather and light, to the immediate foreground. Going from the top to the bottom of the picture you have in your head may be a good way to help the structure.

To provide this detail the setting(s) could be explored through a variety of senses.

Of a person: consider describing in detail: the person's physical qualities; what they wear; how they move, speak and react; any mannerisms; your/the character's reaction to them; their reaction to you. Some background information, for example where they live or work, may be appropriate too.

Of an event/journey: as with a story, readers need to be able to picture their surroundings of the event/journey: appropriate setting details may range from the overview, such as weather and light, to the immediate foreground.

To provide this detail the setting(s) could be explored through a variety of senses.

Some character development may be appropriate. For example, reactions to the event/journey and the reactions of any other character(s) within.

Non-fiction

News report; report or study drawing conclusions; information pamphlet; blog post; informing of an issue and making recommendations; a persuasive speech/essay; a written argument; a letter of complaint or recommendation.

Be sure that you understand the issue in the task, the point of the writing and your audience/reader (other than your marker).

A clear understanding and knowledge of the subject matter should underpin the writing. Check that you have enough ideas about, and information on, the topic.

Points should be well-explained, with supporting evidence or anecdotal reference where appropriate. Facts, statistics and anecdotes, however, can be made up as long as they are believable and convincing.

Generally, a range of persuasive writing techniques should be used in a moderate way. However, if the form and purpose of the task is specifically persuasive (for example, letter, speech, blog post), then a wide range of persuasive writing techniques should be evident and used in a forceful way.

See samples later in this section for further guidance.

Structure

The **structure** of the essay or creative writing should show evidence of clear planning and sequencing of ideas.

Care should be taken to ensure that the piece is not disjointed and that ideas are clearly connected.

Paragraph breaks should be used purposefully and the progression of ideas within and between each paragraph should be fluent.

Paper 2: Writing Practice Paper Answers

To deliver aspects of structure strongly, these pointers might be helpful:

Fiction

Story

The overall shape of the story should be clear and evident, with a strong opening and a purposeful end in mind. It could embrace the use of flashback; it could be a snapshot of a moment in time.

Candidates should show off their ability to write an interesting and manageable narrative with appropriate crisis and shape. There should be sufficient balance between the plot, the description of the characters within it and the setting.

Description

The structure of descriptive writing should be clearly evident.

The lens or viewpoint may zoom out, then in; zoom in, then out; move from the background to the foreground; from the foreground to the background; move from top to bottom.

Of a place: the writer's viewpoint should be established, whether describing a landscape in an organised way from a static position or as if passing through it.

Of a person: the structure should be planned carefully once the appropriate character elements to be described have been decided. There are different ways to describe a person. Consider where the character is.

Of an event/journey: again, once the task has been fully understood, the viewpoint should be established. Is the narrator within or observing the action? Is it best told in chronological order or, for example, by highlighting the different senses or emotions experienced?

Non-fiction

News report; report or study drawing conclusions; information pamphlet; blog post; informing of an issue and making recommendations; a persuasive speech/essay; a written argument; a letter of complaint or recommendation.

Generally, the structure of the writing needs:

- a clear and impactful introduction which explains the issue/topic
- paragraphs to include grouped points – one- or two-sided, depending on the task
- a strong conclusion which sums up the preceding points. Depending on the task it may be relevant to state your own opinion in the conclusion (for example, forms of persuasive writing)
- a topic/focus sentence which should be used clearly at the beginning of each paragraph, with ensuing ideas clearly grouped
- the use of signpost words, such as fronted adverbials, as these may be important to enable the reader to understand the direction of the writing.

Note: If writing a formal letter, a date and correct sign off is always expected.

Register, voice and perspective

The **register** means the degree of formality or informality in the writing. Your 'audience' will help you to decide this.

The **voice** means who you are as the writer/narrator.

The **perspective** means your point of view as the writer/narrator.

As before, think whether you are entertaining, informing, explaining, advising, discussing or persuading as this will impact on your choice of register, voice and perspective. Each task will need to be considered individually so that you write with the appropriate level of formality for the task and audience, and also with the appropriate voice and perspective.

(Care should be taken with the use of violence, adult issues and innuendo. The use of a humorous tone should be measured and acceptable to all readers.)

Guidance for students, teachers and parents

To deliver aspects of register, voice and perspective strongly, these pointers might be helpful:

Fiction

Register: as this is an exam task, this will be generally formal except when writing dialogue which may be colloquial/informal.

Voice: using the first or third person should be sustained throughout.

Perspective: your writing perspective as the author should be clear and consistent. Characters, too, should be consistent in actions, behaviour and words.

Non-fiction

Register: the degree of formality will depend on the task and your audience. Read the question carefully to determine this.

Voice: this will be objective or subjective, depending on the task. As a general rule, if you are presenting a two-sided piece of writing (for example, discursive) use the passive voice to provide objectivity. If the aim in your writing is to persuade (for example, speech, letter) use the active voice to convey subjectivity.

Perspective: stick to your perspective, as the writer, unless you are asked to present two sides to the topic.

Paper 2: ISEB writing task mark scheme – SPAG and expression

The second mark scheme 'SPAG and expression' shows the necessary skills needed in a graded banding system and is explained below. SPAG refers to **S**pelling, **P**unctuation **A**nd **G**rammar.

Read through the bands, from 1–6 and this will show you how to improve your writing so that you have a confident command of sentence grammar, spelling and punctuation.

SPAG and expression		10 marks per task (Total 20)
Band	Mark	Descriptors
6	9–10	• **spelling** is nearly always accurate
		• a full range of **sentence punctuation** is employed accurately to clarify and inform meaning
		• a full range of **sentence structures** is used effectively, to enhance meaning
		• **expression and vocabulary** are imaginative, precise, idiomatic and controlled
		• use of an appropriate **tense** is sustained throughout, changing only to achieve specific effects successfully
5	7–8	• **spelling** is mostly accurate
		• basic **sentence punctuation** is accurate
		• **expression and vocabulary** are used clearly, precisely and appropriately
		• use of an appropriate **tense** is consistent throughout
4	5–6	• the **spelling** of straightforward words is accurate
		• basic **sentence punctuation** is mostly accurate
		• an attempt to use sophisticated **expression and vocabulary** lacks control/or expression and vocabulary is very straightforward
		• there may some unexplained changing of **tense**

Paper 2: Writing Practice Paper Answers

Band	Mark	Descriptors
3	3–4	• some inaccuracy in the **spelling** of straightforward words • evidence of regular comma-splicing or other errors in basic **sentence punctuation** • **expression** often uncontrolled; **vocabulary** used inappropriately • moves between **tenses** regularly and without explanation
2	2	• **spelling** regularly inaccurate • little command of basic **sentence grammar and punctuation** • a little attempt to articulate ideas • very little control over **tense**
1	1	• an attempt to respond

SPAG and expression

Spelling should be nearly always accurate.

However, do not hold back from using adventurous vocabulary, even if you are unsure how to spell it.

The spelling of commonly used words should be accurate.

Copy words within the title/task carefully.

Sentence punctuation: The best candidates will use commas, semicolons, colons, dashes, brackets and apostrophes with confidence. Dialogue, where used, should be punctuated and laid out accurately.

Try to show off a range of punctuation to prove that you know how to use it to best effect.

Sentence structures should provide a variety of openings, as appropriate, in both fiction and non-fiction.

In fiction, they prevent the writing from becoming monotonous and in non-fiction they may guide the reader. Simple, compound and complex sentences should be used appropriately and smoothly according to the context.

Controlled sentence punctuation is impressive and will aid clarity and meaning. The best complex sentences are thought out in your head before writing. Know where your sentence ends.

Expression, in this context, means a careful choice of words to write in the tone, degree of formality or style needed for the task.

A sophisticated, relevant and succinct **vocabulary** will set apart the best candidates.

A strong, well-chosen word will do the job of several weak words. Be aware of shades of meaning between words and find the best one for the job.

The use of inappropriate slang and modern euphemisms should be avoided.

With practice and thinking about expression and vocabulary, you will find your own writing voice.

Verb **tenses** should be used accurately and consistently and tense changes used for effect where appropriate. For example, use a flashback as a stylistic device in fiction writing. Check that you do not move from the past to the present tense in the exciting part of the story where you are 'living it' with your characters.

The natural way to write seems to be in the past tense so if you choose to write the whole essay in the present tense (for example, description) be careful to sustain it.

Non-fiction writing may include a range of tenses within one essay, for example: 'You will find ...'; 'Many people think that ...'; 'The evidence proved that ...'

Sample responses to a range of writing styles and forms

In the following section you will find sample questions, plans and responses for typical Writing Paper questions. The writing samples represented are: narrative, descriptive, persuasive, discursive, letter, blog and report.

The Writing Paper tasks will invite many different responses; our samples provide just one way of interpreting each example question. Each individual response in the exam will reflect the candidate's own voice and personality.

There is one Writing Paper mark scheme for 'Ideas, structure, form and voice' and one for 'SPAG and expression'. These mark schemes are used for all titles and forms and can be found earlier in this section. Combined, they award marks for the big picture (addressing the question, ideas, structure, form and purpose) and technical focus and expression (use of appropriate vocabulary and language techniques, accuracy in spelling, punctuation and grammar). The samples show how a good level can be achieved within each form of writing by including the features relevant to it and by communicating ideas clearly, accurately and imaginatively.

Each essay has its own plan. This is an essential part of the writing process as it will provide a sense of purpose and direction and frees up the mind so that the written response can be deliberately crafted. Different methods of planning are shown – personal preference and suitability for each writing question will determine which type of plan is favoured or chosen as most appropriate. Plans should be brief and in note form to save time.

Each sample response is annotated. While these annotations are not exhaustive, they are good indicators of the skills and features which should be demonstrated within each particular form of writing.

There are two opportunities to shine in the Writing Paper. Under exam conditions there may not be time to write two essays of this length, but these sample responses each show a best effort, which gives something to aim for.

Sample balanced discussion question and response

Question

> 'Children, not adults, should decide how much screen time to enjoy.'
> Write an article for your school magazine in which you discuss this statement and give your views.

(This question is taken from Writing Practice Paper 3 on page 69.)

Plan

Para 1: Intro

Screen time is much discussed in today's changing technological world

Para 2: Children should decide

- Better understanding
- Know what they want to watch/do on screen with examples
- Can be sensible/mature about viewing
- Know how to lead healthy life
- Adult may be too strict/over-reduce time

Para 3: Adults should decide

- Adult could be more aware of pitfalls/more responsible
- Parent wiser: sees overall picture, better placed for healthy, balanced decision
- Adults better awareness of time, children get caught up in game and lose track of time, can be addictive
- Choice of screen time – unsuitable/peer pressure

Paper 2: Writing Practice Paper Answers

Para 4: Conclusion

- Screen time discussion: two ways
- Flexible/consider holidays
- Open discussion

Sample response

1 Para 1 Intro: uses task words/establishes parameters of task.

[1]Screen time is much discussed today both in society and amongst children and adults in our school.[2] We live in an age of rapidly expanding technology, with new and exciting ways to tempt young and old to spend their leisure time viewing a screen. But who should decide how much time to allow children for this? Is a child more up to date with current trends and so best to determine their own screen time? Or is an adult the best judge of how much spare time should be spent on screen?[3]

2 Relates to task/establishes audience.

3 A triple of rhetorical questions leads into Para 2.

4 Para 2: topic sentence/clear connective to open section on child's view.

5 Pronoun 'us' includes/draws in the reader.

7 Use of complex sentence which includes a list.

10 Repetition of sentence structure for effect/emphasis on child's perspective.

Firstly,[4] let us[5] consider children making the decision about the amount of leisure screen time.[6] Children are well aware of the wide range of entertainment out there to enjoy[7]: messaging friends, watching YouTube, watching TV or films, playing puzzle computer games or 'shooter' games, interacting with TV influenced games or life games creating new worlds and characters.[8] Therefore, they are best placed to decide what they want to do and watch on screen. They are in the hotseat.[9] Only they will know when they are satisfied. Only they will know what feels right. Only they will know how best to spend leisure time.[10] Children can be sensible and mature both about screen time and making choices for a healthy lifestyle balance. They may fear an adult could be too strict and overly reduce screen time.[11]

6 Impartial/formal tone – no bias in discussion paragraphs.

8 Detail/knowledge of subject area.

9 Short sentence/metaphor to gain reader's attention.

11 Structure to link to next paragraphs.

12 Para 3: important sentence opener – shows structure giving the opposing adult's view.

13 Using task words – shows still on task.

On the other hand,[12] looking at it from the adult's point of view[13], they may take a more objective, responsible position.[14] Adults are the onlookers: they see the overall picture and they will spot when children are looking tired from going to bed too late. They may see them lose a healthy glow from the outdoor life. They may see them lose interest in hobbies and more energetic activities in favour of a life in front of a screen. In addition,[15] they have a perspective on real time. Children may get caught up in a game, certain they know when to stop, only for a friend to join in and for the addictive nature of the game to take hold for longer. They may be under the influence of peer pressure and manipulative game creators.[16]

14 Long sentence containing subordinate clause – showing off good level of punctuation.

15 Sustained use of clear connective sentence openers.

16 Each paragraph of discussion has ordered/structured ideas, from plan.

142

Sample responses to a range of writing styles and forms

17 Para 4 Conclusion: refers to task words.

My view,[17] on this contentious[18] issue, is that mutual understanding and discussion of the enjoyment and risks of screen time must be the answer. Children can educate adults on the different kinds of activities they enjoy and alleviate their fears, whilst adults can expand a child's views with wise, well-meant words.[19] Adults may therefore agree to time spent on puzzle games, or a SpongeBob SquarePants game, but deny any add-on purchases that go with the games. Also, they may decide to limit 'shooter' games by age-appropriateness.[20] With open discussion the adult and child can mutually agree time boundaries, with flexibility across term and holiday times. A bit of give-and-take on both sides can result in a win-win situation, with more harmony on this topic within our school community.

18 Precise/mature vocabulary.

19 Alliteration – repetition of 'w' sound emphasises the view being presented.

20 Facts/technical knowledge of task.

(For more guidance, refer to the mark scheme on page 135 onwards.)

Sample report question and response
Question

Write a report drawing conclusions about an environmental or ecological issue in your local area.

(This question is taken from Writing Practice Paper 4 on page 69.)

Plan
Para 1: Intro – explain location, time, purpose of report

Para 2/3: Pondlife – life in and on the ponds

Para 4: Trees

Para 5: Human activity – walkers, dogs, pond dippers, school visits

Para 6: Conclusion – sum up/advice/measures to help protect the woodland site

Sample response

1 Subheading used for clarity/accessibility.

Location and focus of interest[1]

The area under focus comprises two ponds surrounded by woodland on three sides with a busy road to the immediate east of the larger pond. There is a well-used public footpath between the two ponds.[2] The point of the report is to survey the whole area over a period from dawn to dusk in early April and to assess the impact of human activity on the ecological diversity of the area. The report concludes with advice for both individuals and the local council.[3]

2 Location established.

3 Purpose of report established in line with task.

Pondlife

At the time of survey, the pond was full of water,[4] although it is known to dry out in summer months. Within the ponds there is evidence of fish, water boatman, newts (including the protected Great Crested Newt) frogs and toads.

4 Time and place established.

Paper 2: Writing Practice Paper Answers

Waterlilies, reeds and the rare starfruit plant are features of the larger pond.[5] It was noted that[6] towards dusk, toads and frogs, then coming out of hibernation in nearby gardens, made their way to the pond often over the road which has a steady flow of traffic.

The ponds are home to a variety of waterfowl[7] and it was obvious that nest building was beginning. During the survey, a heron came for a short time to hunt for fish. The surrounding trees provide a safe habitat for several species of birds including woodpeckers and rooks.[8]

Trees

The ponds are surrounded mainly by sapling and mature oak trees. The acorn drop therefore attracts squirrels which do not seem to interfere with the pond or birdlife.[9]

Human activity

Fine weather on the survey day increased human activity.[10] Walkers largely kept to the path between the ponds. It was noted, however, that some dogs were allowed to swim in the ponds and chase the nesting water birds. Several children arrived to pond dip. Some remained on the edge of the water to take samples; some waded into deeper water. It was difficult to see whether samples were returned to the water. It was disappointing to see that a school party which arrived in the afternoon showed little respect for the habitat.[11]

Conclusions

[12]The ecology of the area is diverse but is at risk[13] due to the footfall of adults, children and dogs and passing motorists. These measures are advised:[14]

- Signage around the ponds should[15] be introduced to discourage dog owners from allowing their dogs to swim in the pond or disturb the wildfowl.
- Signage along the roadside should be put up to warn[16] motorists about toads and frogs crossing.
- An information board should be constructed to promote knowledge of the wildlife in the area and to show the fragility[17] of the existing ecosystem.
- Schoolchildren should be taught how to pond dip without destroying any creatures or their habitat. Large groups should ideally be accompanied and instructed by a wildlife ranger.
- Local schools should have access to free informative talks from volunteer rangers. Poster competitions will encourage their interest and understanding.[18]

By taking these small steps, the ecology[19] of this beautiful area can then be preserved for, and enjoyed by, all creatures great and small.[20]

(For more guidance, refer to the mark scheme on page 135 onwards.)

---

5 Evidence of good knowledge of subject matter.

6 Passive voice to provide objectivity.

7 Clear topic sentence.

8 Detail/knowledge of subject area and factual evidence.

9 Sentences straightforward, clear and not too long.

10 Strong, unbiased opening sentence.

11 Inference throughout paragraph: human activity is adversely affecting the ecology.

12 Statement to sum up.

13 Emotive language for impact.

14 Refers back to question wording; recommendations are clearly laid out using bullet points.

15 Strong advice – 'should' indicates obligation.

16 Emotive verb used for impact.

17 Emphasises the need for action in a balanced sentence.

18 Examples of manageable and enjoyable activities to give advice and promote awareness.

19 Uses words from the question wording.

20 Ends on positive note using an idiom relating to nature.

Sample responses to a range of writing styles and forms

Sample narrative question and response

Question

'We were lucky indeed that day.' Use this sentence as the last line of a story.

(This question is taken from Writing Practice Paper 5 on page 70.)

Plan

Para 1: short introductory paragraph to describe setting, weather and mood. First person/past tense

Para 2: opening – describe car, setting, excited mood

Para 3: development – tone/mood changes. Setting details. Dialogue. Arrival of elephants

Para 4: crisis – elephant prepares to charge. Show not tell/questions/short sentences – fear

Para 5: resolution – escape as car can turn and twist more easily. Describe escape. Fear/relief

Para 6: very short closing sentence to go full circle

Sample response

The sun beat down from the relentless, blue, Malawian sky. We counted ourselves lucky – a perfect day for a safari. Or so we thought.[1]

The engine of our car, which seemed small compared to the vast landscape, spluttered[2] into action. The noise cut through, and seemed to insult,[3] the silence of the early morning. But we had no choice. To walk would have been foolhardy. As we carefully followed the map, the miles of dusty dirt tracks trailed[4] behind us. We were excited, feeling certain that we would strike gold that day and see for ourselves, in the flesh, those magnificent wild beasts that inhabited that part of Malawi. The car, which had seemed at first to be an incongruous and ugly lump of metal, became our friend as it took us on our quest.[5]

It was not long before the trail led into woodland.[6] But this was no ordinary wood with welcoming dappled shade and shadows whispering over glades and ferns.[7] Instead a dense canopy climbed, clung and clambered so that soon the light was struggling to find a way through the tangled mass of vegetation.[8]

'Keep your eyes peeled. We may be lucky here,' urged my father.

It took a while for our eyes to become accustomed to the gloom and, rounding a corner, we were slow to see on the path ahead two grey hulks looming towards us out of the dark green shadows.[9]

'Elephants! A mother and calf. Camera! Quick!'[10]

1 Para 1: short opening paragraph to establish setting (triple) and mood/problem hinted at.

2 Para 2: focus sentence – importance of car. Onomatopoeic verb – car's engine can be heard.

3 Personification – shows noise of engine in contrast to the peace of the morning.

4 Example of varied sentence openers. Alliteration to pull words together and provide detail.

5 Strong vocabulary. Personification of car – foreshadows that it will help them to escape.

6 Para 3: focus sentence to introduce new setting.

7 Soft vocabulary choices which include personification and onomatopoeia.

8 Alliteration/triple/harsher sounds to create contrast.

9 Long sentence including relative and subordinate clauses to give detail.

10 Short sentences within dialogue to show excitement.

145

Paper 2: Writing Practice Paper Answers

12 Simile to provide image of huge ears.	But when I looked through the viewfinder, sweat broke out on my forehead and panic pulsed through my veins.[11] The larger animal's ears moved forward, like two enormous synchronised doors[12] and, at the same time, its trunk rose imperiously into the air. My questioning eyes met my father's. We had a snap decision to make now; a snapshot was not an option.[13] Reverse? Not powerful or quick enough. Swing sideways? Too much undergrowth, left and right, to trap us. Only one way. Forward.[14]
13 Balanced statements and use of semicolon; includes a play on words.	
15 Para 5: focus sentence shifts to elephant.	[15]As the enraged elephant lifted one enormous foot in preparation for the charge – a foot that on its own could annihilate us and our car – my father jammed the gear stick into first and accelerated straight ahead. I noticed, his strained body position and clenched white knuckles[16] on the steering wheel and in that same fleeting second I saw fragments of my whole life cascade, splinter and fall around me like the shards of a glass mirror.[17]
18 Strong verbs/onomatopoeia.	The noise of the revving engine and the trumpeting of the elephant[18] overpowered all other sensations but technology outwitted nature's brute force[19] and we sped past too quickly for the animal's lumbering sideways turn. Without speaking we hurtled on. Through the wood, through the scrub and bush, through the undergrowth until we were out once more under the scorching, searing sun.[20] Relief washed over us leaving every sinew and muscle weak.[21]
20 Repetition and list-like effect to show speed/detail.	
22 Para 6: use of task sentence/in para of own/goes full circle with opening.	We were lucky indeed that day.[22]

11 Para 4: show not tell introduces crisis/panic.

14 Combination of questions, answers and short sentences show breathlessness/fear/tension.

16 Show not tell to describe physical effect of fear.

17 Triple/simile/strong vocabulary choices to show extreme fear.

19 Personification to emphasise how the car comes to their rescue.

21 Contrasting feeling – show not tell.

(For more guidance, refer to the mark scheme on page 135 onwards.)

Sample letter giving recommendations question and response

Question

Your school wants to appoint a 'Kindness Monitor' whose job it will be to try to help the school towards a culture of kindness.
Write a letter to your headteacher, recommending why you think you should be appointed and what things you might do.

(This question is taken from Writing Practice Paper 6 on page 70.)

Plan

Para 1: Intro: introduce me, ideas, recognising others will apply

Para 2: why me: history at school + e.g. new girl Sam

Para 3: ideas: K badge/committee, drop in centre, letterbox

Para 4: reduce my time for fun? Kindness normal, strong persuasive end

Sample responses to a range of writing styles and forms

Sample response

6th June 2022[1]

Dear Mrs Henry,[2]

I am writing to recommend myself for the role of 'Kindness Monitor'.[3] I consider that I have the qualities of a kind person necessary for the position. Additionally, I have many ideas about what could be done within our school community to support those in need of help and to promote kindness.[4] I appreciate that many pupils, like me, will be keen to be appointed to this role so I ask that you please read my letter with consideration.[5]

Firstly,[6] I hope that I have shown that I am, mostly, a kind and sympathetic pupil.[7] Now that I am nearing the end of Year 7 and moving into my final year at our school, you can look back at my time here and recall[8] examples of my thoughtful acts. In Year 5, Sam joined our school and initially she was shy, but I chatted to her at lunch and invited her into our games at playtime, and now she is a confident and popular member of Year 7. Another example[9] was earlier this year, when a friend of mine was having a tough time at home. As we walked home at the end of the day, I hope I was able to give her the hand of friendship and make her smile.[10] Added to this is the fact that I am the oldest of my three siblings. I had to find my own way through. So I have had practice in suggesting to my brother and sister how acts of kindness can go a long way and help situations.[11]

In addition, the ideas I have to help a culture of kindness within our school begin with the role of 'Monitor'.[12] It may be that more than one monitor will be needed in Years 6, 7 and 8. So we could form a committee or small team, where we share ideas and support each other. I would suggest a member of staff could oversee the meetings and be there to turn to. Each of these monitors could wear a badge, with a 'K' for 'Kindness' on it.[13] If there is a pupil who is seeking a listening ear, for instance about a playground incident, or falling out with a friend, or a problem in class, they can look for the 'K' symbol. They will be assured that they will be listened to and helped. Furthermore, we could have a 'Drop in Centre' at certain times of the week (with a letterbox outside for urgent requests)[14] in case anyone wants a quiet time to chat to another child who is trustworthy and understanding.[15]

In conclusion, I hope my application for the role of a Kindness Monitor, and my ideas, will act as a positive force within our school.[16] I have thought about the implications of wearing a 'K' badge, and wondered whether

Annotations:

- **1** Letter format needs date.
- **2** Letter format needs who you are writing to.
- **3** Para 1 Intro: responds to question, uses key task words.
- **4** Addressing audience/purpose/setting out letter intentions.
- **5** Formal tone – appropriate register for task.
- **6** Para 2: signpost sentence opener – first set of recommendations.
- **7** Topic sentence – what this paragraph will be about.
- **8** Formal vocabulary to sustain formal tone; also uses direct address ('you') to engage reader.
- **9** Helpful vocabulary to introduce examples.
- **10** Details/examples to recommend self – engages the reader.
- **11** Leads into next paragraph – sequencing/structure.
- **12** Para 3: opens with task words/still on task – leads into second set of recommendations.
- **13** Persuasive ideas – provides detail.
- **14** Use of brackets – range of punctuation.
- **15** Emotive vocabulary to do with kindness – achieves purpose.
- **16** Para 4 Conclusion: persuasion targeted at audience – achieves purpose.

147

Paper 2: Writing Practice Paper Answers

17 Rhetorical question – adds depth to letter writer's thoughts and voice.

being a role model might mean being able to have less fun myself?[17] But I think not. Kindness must seem to be normal, typical and achievable[18] for all. I hope that in recommending these ideas, I have proved I am a strong candidate for this role. I would not let you down.[19]

18 Triple/rule of three for emphasis.

19 Strong ending to leave impact on headteacher.

20 Sign off – 'Yours sincerely' as addressed to a specific name.

Yours sincerely,[20]

Ben Sousa

(For more guidance, refer to the mark scheme on page 135 onwards.)

Sample descriptive question and response

Question

Write a description of a scene where the weather plays an important role.

(This question is taken from Writing Practice Paper 7 on page 71.)

Plan

Para 1: first person/past tense/good weather/falling asleep on beach/calm mood

Para 2: I hear and see storm approaching/feeling anxious

Para 3: rain/people scrambling to pack up belongings/lightning/panic/racing to cars

Para 4: effects of the storm on the sea/beach

Para 5: watch in awe as the storm moves on/describe effect on the scene/calm mood

Sample response

1 Para 1: perspective of narrator, place, mood all established.

[1]As I lay on the soft sand with the sun warmly embracing me[2] and the sea, cool and refreshing, gently lapping nearby, I thought how peaceful the world could be. Slowly my limbs relaxed, settling into the welcoming sand. Before long,[3] I was drifting into sleep as the happy sounds of the beach seemed to recede[4] into the distance.

[5]It was a quiet, but threatening, rumble that disturbed my dream. The rumble became a menacing grumble[6] and, blinking upwards,[7] I saw huge black clouds gathering like an army on the horizon. My heart beat faster.[8] How soon

2 Personification of the sun to show nature is a friend at this point.

3 Good range of sentence starters.

4 Vocabulary choices – strong verb.

5 Para 2: a change of mood.

6 Onomatopoeia – to provide the sound of the growing thunder.

7 Good use of subordinate clauses to bring detail to description.

8 Short sentence to bring tension.

148

Sample responses to a range of writing styles and forms

9 Rhetorical question adds to feeling of uncertainty.

10 Para 3: storm arrives and chaos described.

11 Use of dashes and commas to add detail and create sense of urgency.

14 Repetition – to emphasise the movement and panic.

15 Para 4: effect of storm on sea/beach.

18 Para 5: passing storm's effect on narrator and the scene.

19 Short and incomplete sentences convey anxiety.

[9]would this storm envelop and overpower me and the other holiday-makers?

[10]Then the rain started – just a few huge drops to start with – and the previous calm mood was shattered. Clothes were pulled on haphazardly, towels shaken and rammed into bags already bulging, and buckets retrieved from the water's edge.[11] Against the darkening sky there was a sudden flash of bright white light.[12] The heavens were torn apart with one almighty crash. Children shrieked, frightened dogs yelped and adults screamed commands.[13] Then running. Everyone was running. Over the sand, over the pebbles and over the slippery seaweed to the safety of their cars.[14]

[15]The waves no longer lapped gently. They too were caught up in the battle. Sudden and strong gusts of wind tussled with them and they fought back, tossing and turning and creating crests[16] of unruly white foam. Spewing their contents onto and up the beach, the waves were then sucked back, gathering more ammunition for the next attack.[17]

[18]Now I was alone. The only one to witness nature's power.[19] Hunched and huddled, I watched and waited as the storm's anger gradually peaked and then abated.[20] The battle was won here: it was time to move on and find another helpless victim. It was not long before the only sounds to be heard were the gentle, rhythmical lapping of the waves and the call of the seagulls that were enjoying the spoils and pickings on the war-torn beach.[21]

12 Assonance – to pull the monosyllabic words together so that the sharp sounds stand out.

13 Strong verbs – onomatopoeia to create sound effects.

16 Alliteration – to emphasise 's', 't' and 'cr' for sea sound effects.

17 Metaphors – to provide battle images.

20 Good balance of elements in this sentence – pairs like 'watched and waited'.

21 Longer sentence with soft vocabulary choices to re-establish calm.

(For more guidance, refer to the mark scheme on page 135 onwards.)

Sample blog question and response
Question

Write a blog about an outdoor activity which you enjoy.

(This question is taken from Writing Practice Paper 7 on page 71.)

Plan

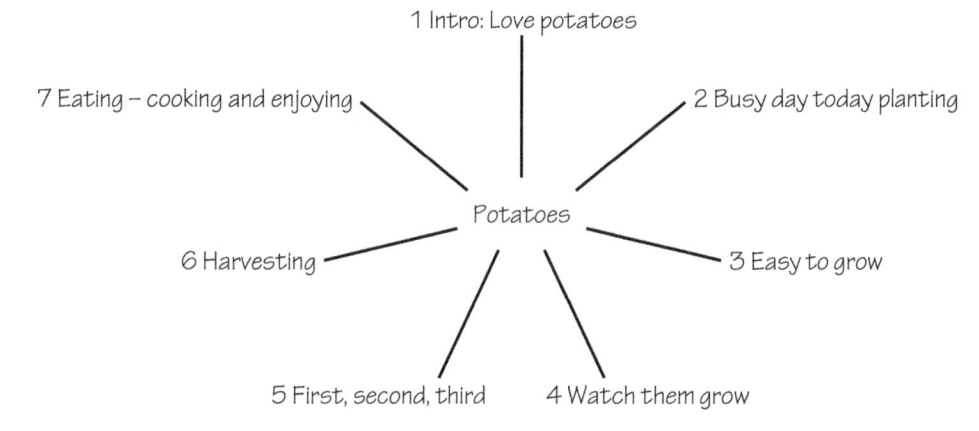

Potatoes
- 1 Intro: Love potatoes
- 2 Busy day today planting
- 3 Easy to grow
- 4 Watch them grow
- 5 First, second, third
- 6 Harvesting
- 7 Eating – cooking and enjoying

149

Paper 2: Writing Practice Paper Answers

Sample response

Life is Delicious[1]

1 A title that catches the reader's eye.

I love potatoes.[2] I always have. I love planting them. I love the anticipation of pulling them up to see how many are there! But most of all, I love eating them. Today is the day when this adventure starts for a new year.[3]

2 Para 1: Personal opinion – written in the first person – main point in first paragraph.

3 Personal opinion expressed in an individual voice; fits audience: young people with interest in gardening.

Dad and I have had a busy day – we planted our potatoes in the garden![4]

4 Written in diary style – documenting day-to-day activities.

5 Interesting way to start a sentence – details follow in subsequent paragraphs.

Typically,[5] I had wanted to plant them last month, but Dad said it was too cold. Apparently in the olden days, gardeners used to say that a good time to plant potatoes was when you could sit on the ground, and not get a cold behind![6]

6 Engages the reader with an amusing anecdote.

7 Short paragraphs with clear topic sentences.

Potatoes are really easy to grow.[7] Today we made the holes for the seed potatoes to go in. There's something about the soil running through your fingers that makes you connect with nature. We just pop one in the ground, cover it with soil, and then wait for it to grow into a big plant.[8]

8 Informal, chatty language.

It's so exciting to go and inspect the beds every week or so, looking for signs of life. When we notice the typical stumpy green shoots poking out of the ground, we know they are on their way. The night times can be quite cold in spring and, if there is a frost, the leaves will wilt, turning an unhealthy pale yellow before going crispy and brown.[9] As a precaution, Dad and I cover the baby plants with sheets of garden fleece to keep them warm.[10]

9 Show rather than tell.

10 Offers reflections and tips.

There are three main categories of potato, and we are trying to grow all of them. 'First earlies' or 'new potatoes' grow the quickest and are harvested when they haven't got to full size. We are also growing 'second earlies', which are a bit bigger and get harvested next and finally some 'main crop' which are the large kind that you would use for baking or roasting.[11]

11 Gives factual information – important feature.

You can always tell when the main crop potatoes are ready, as the plants (at least a metre tall by this point) stop growing and start to die back. Deciding when first and second earlies are ready is much more difficult. There's nothing worse than revisiting week after week, only to harvest the potatoes and find they are still tiny and not worth eating![12]

12 Modest tone – we're all in this together and it can go wrong.

When we get it right though, there's nothing like the taste of delicious lightly boiled spuds, fresh from the ground.[13] The first earlies have that welcome taste of

13 Follows plan structure: planting, harvesting, eating/'delicious' refers back to title.

Sample responses to a range of writing styles and forms

14 Idiom – informal language/alliteration of 't' sound emphasises phrase and enjoyment.

spring that tickle your tastebuds,[14] but because they are immature and haven't had a chance to grow a thick, protective skin, they don't last very long before going bad. That is music to my ears, as it gives me an excuse to slather them with butter and chopped chives. My mouth is watering now just thinking about them.

I wonder how much longer I will have to wait? How do you like yours?[15]

15 Ending: rhetorical question/catchy to engage the reader and invite a response.

(For more guidance, refer to the mark scheme on page 135 onwards.)

Sample persuasive speech question and response
Question

'Boredom is beneficial'
Write a speech, for or against this statement, to deliver to your school assembly. Try to be as persuasive as you can.

(This question is taken from Writing Practice Paper 9 on page 72.)

Plan

Para 1: Intro – title as starting point/anecdote/explain topic and point of view

Para 2: Hobbies, exercise

Para 3: Inventions/ideas need time

Para 4: Learning how to use time – teaches resilience, independence

Para 5: Conclusion – end strongly

Sample response

1 Para 1: a strong start – uses the title, turning it into a rhetorical question and clearly indicating this is an argument 'for'.

2 Anecdote/personal experience/and use of personal pronouns 'you' and 'your' to engage reader/school audience.

4 Triple/rule of three used in short sentences for impact.

7 Statistic introduced to support argument.

Is boredom beneficial? Yes, it absolutely is![1] And I'll tell you why. Imagine it's Sunday afternoon. You have finished your homework, outside it's wet and cold and your brother and sister are out. 'I've got nothing to do,' you whine. 'I'm so bored.'[2] It's as if you feel you should be entertained. Why? Would you like to be responsible for keeping someone else occupied all day?[3] Probably not. So let's rethink this situation. Let's remove the negativity. Let's spin the coin.[4] Instead of saying, 'I'm so bored,' why not think to yourself, 'Hooray, I've got some time to myself! Now, how shall I use it?'

Perhaps you could take up a new hobby?[5] Try your hand at some sort of craft or model-making? Or you could immerse yourself in a great book so that you are whisked off to other places and times which fire your imagination.[6] If those pursuits are too sedentary, you could devise a new exercise routine using props and obstacles from around the house and garden. Then set yourself time targets to achieve greater fitness. Let's say you spend three hours doing new things instead of moping around, then that would be 20% of your day spent positively.[7]

3 Plays on feelings of guilt persuasively.

5 Para 2: topic sentence, posed as a question to draw in audience.

6 Strong vocabulary, especially verbs, to engage/inspire.

151

Paper 2: Writing Practice Paper Answers

9 Good use of semicolon; extended metaphor strengthens the message to audience.

10 Passionate emotive vocabulary/use of exaggeration for effect.

12 Para 4: topic sentence featuring strong vocabulary and a triple for emphasis.

14 Repetition of strong, emotive vocabulary to drive point home.

15 Para 5: topic sentence introduces conclusion and personal opinion.

17 Most important word placed at the end of the sentence for impact.

19 Speech goes full circle by returning to original anecdote.

Have you ever wondered how many great inventions were discovered because the inventor was bored or, to put it another way, had time to think things out?[8] Uncluttered time can be very creative; ideas need time to take root, germinate and grow.[9] Just imagine, you might be the next great inventor acclaimed globally for your invaluable help to humanity.[10] Space travel, the internet, mobile phones – all this technology started in someone's head and the next big thing could be in your head![11]

But perhaps the most important thing about knowing how to fill time alone is that it teaches you independence, self-reliance and self-knowledge.[12] By learning to do things on your own, you work out what makes you happy. Win, win! Like a form of mindfulness, really.[13] Once you have the knack, you'll crave 'boredom'; crave[14] having time to spend on your own so that you can pursue new ideas or new hobbies.

So, to conclude, I believe[15] that we should find a new positive word to replace the negative[16] noun 'boredom'. Boredom actually can bring energy, creativity, innovation. Boredom means that you have that precious commodity – time.[17] 'Keeping busy?' you are asked as if that's a good state to be in. 'No,' you can now reply. 'I've got time to myself and I love it.'[18] Next Sunday afternoon[19] when you momentarily think you are bored, don't give in. Be energised, enlightened and enthused.[20]

8 Para 3: topic sentence including relative clause, introduces next point in argument – again in question form.

11 Repetition and listing to engage reader/listener add detail to argument; exclamation mark used for emphasis.

13 Incomplete/short sentences and chatty tone as if author in conversation with audience.

16 Use of opposites.

18 Dialogue to provide realism; allows another verbal texture to argument.

20 Use of imperative, triple/rule of three, alliteration, powerful vocabulary to end with strong 'call to action' to school assembly.

(For more guidance, refer to the mark scheme on page 135 onwards.)

Appendix: Subject content from ISEB English 13+ specification

The following selected text, direct from the ISEB English 13+ specification, explains what candidates are expected to know and understand, and outlines the breakdown and content of the Reading and Writing Papers.

You may like to read the document in full at:
www.iseb.co.uk/Schools/Examination-syllabuses-specimen-papers/New-CE-at-13

13+ Subject content

Reading

Text choices for the examination papers are taken from literary texts, fiction and non-fiction, appropriate in language, style and content to the age/interest range. An introductory line of explanation may precede the text, to give necessary context. Certain words may be glossed.

A Foundation reading paper is provided for pupils who are developing the skills and vocabulary required for Paper 1. The paper may be used for assessment at 13+ by agreement with senior schools, or to support learning in Years 6 and 7. Text choices on the Foundation paper take the form of a prose passage.

Paper 1 reading texts may take the form of a prose passage, a poem or an excerpt from a play, and will be selected at the setters' discretion without any standard pattern. This is to encourage the study of a variety of texts in Years 7 and 8, and different approaches to the development of reading skills.

Candidates should be able to:

- select information which can be obtained from a careful reading of the passage
- understand the literal meaning of complex sentences, facilitated by a command of sentence grammar
- display a working knowledge of syntax, punctuation, the main parts of speech and representation of voice; for example, subject, object, verb, noun, pronoun, adjective, adverb, phrase, subordinate clause, preposition, direct and reported speech, narrative voice (first/third person)
- access, understand and respond to deeper (secondary) meanings
- summarise ideas and meanings in their own words
- supply answers, giving explanation and reasoning
- provide evidence from the text for more complex points of understanding
- explain vocabulary in context: respond to meanings within their immediate context and within the context of the whole text
- say why or how language is used in a particular way, exploring the effects of language choices
- show how the form of the writing impacts on meaning
- make an evaluative response
- structure a logical argument in response to a discussion question on the text, using a model such as the 'Point Explanation Evidence Analysis' model.

Writing

Paper 2 is designed to assess the writing skills of candidates at all levels.

Candidates should be able to:

- write in a full range of styles, including narrative, descriptive, informative, discursive, persuasive
- employ the appropriate form, for example: a story; a description; a news report; a report or study drawing conclusions; an information pamphlet or blog post, informing the audience of an issue and making recommendations; a speech or debate of an issue; a written argument; a letter of complaint or recommendation
- adopt a style and register appropriate to the task; use a range of appropriate expression and vocabulary

Appendix

- make clear use of prompts and follow instructions
- plan their writing, so that it is clearly structured; make use of paragraphs
- show command of accurate sentence grammar, spelling and punctuation.

Assessment objective

Candidates may take EITHER the Foundation (Reading) paper OR Paper 1 (Reading).

ALL candidates take Paper 2 (Writing).

CE at 13+	Marks
Either Foundation (Reading)	50: 1 hour 10 minutes
Or Paper 1 (Reading)	50: 1 hour 10 minutes
Plus Paper 2 (Writing)	50: 1 hour 15 minutes

Foundation (Reading)

This paper assesses understanding of an unseen prose passage.

		Marks
Section A	Eight multiple choice questions, to direct candidates' understanding of the text: questions test information selection, command of more complex meanings, grammar, vocabulary and idiom.	15
Section B	Questions invite a more developed response to the meanings of the text and effects of language.	25
Section C	A directed writing question inviting candidates to respond empathically and imaginatively to the passage, while testing their command and use of the information available.	10

Paper 1 (Reading)

This paper assesses understanding of an unseen text, which may be prose, poetry or drama.

		Marks
Section A	Eight multiple choice questions, testing command of grammatical meaning, vocabulary, idiom and the selection of information.	15
Section B	Questions of graded difficulty, designed to test deeper understanding: inference, response to the effects of language, imagery and form, and command of meaning in context. Candidates should respond in full sentences, selecting quotation and giving explanation to support their ideas, where indicated.	25
Section C	Continuing directly from Section B: a 10-mark question requiring an extended written response to the whole text. This should be clearly structured and developed across three paragraphs of argument, using a model such as the Point Explanation Evidence Analysis model. Each paragraph should begin with a clear topic sentence, stating the point of argument, and develop with explanation and discussion of evidence; stronger candidates will include analysis of the effects of language and form.	10

Appendix

Paper 2 (Writing)

The paper provides opportunity for **all** candidates to demonstrate their writing skills. Candidates choose **TWO** options from a choice of four, which may include: narrative writing; a descriptive piece or report on a journey, event or person; a persuasive speech; a letter discussing an issue and making recommendations to the reader.

		Marks
Response	clear use of prompts	30
	effective organisation and structuring of ideas	
	use of features appropriate to purpose and form	
	appropriate use of perspective, voice and register	
Language	spelling	20
	sentence punctuation	
	variety of sentence structures	
	use of expression and vocabulary: imaginative, precise, idiomatic and controlled	
	consistent use of tense	